Crossing the Rainbow Bridge

The joy is in the journey and the journey never ends!

Colleen Nicholson

Crossing the Rainbow Bridge

Animal Journeys to Heaven

Colleen Nicholson
Animal Communicator

Carp Cove Press
Liverpool, New York

Requests for permission should be addressed to:
Carp Cove Press
P.O. Box 2991
Liverpool, NY 13089-2991 U.S.A.
Orders taken at: CarpCovePress@holisticanimal.com
http://holisticanimal.com

Colleen Nicholson
    Crossing the Rainbow Bridge: Animal Journeys to Heaven
    First Edition

Graphic Design: Colleen Kiefer
Editor: Kathy Hill
Cover Art and Jacket Design: Lisa McLaughlin
Prepress Production: Vance Blackburn

Library of Congress Catalog Number: 00-191973

ISBN: 0-9703752-4-7
Carp Cove Press

Printed in the United States of America

Dedication

*This book is respectfully dedicated to
the countless animals loved and lost,
and to the grieving humans they left behind.
May we all find comfort in having loved them truly,
and may they have found hope in mankind.*

Acknowledgments

I would like to offer my deepest gratitude to every person and animal written about within the pages of this book. By so graciously allowing me to be your interpreter, you have touched my heart with your stories and changed my life. "Thank you" seems hardly enough – immortalizing you in print I find more fitting.

My heartfelt thanks and gratitude go to my parents, who always made sure during my youth that I had a companion dog by my side and an appreciation for all animals in life; Louise Vespa, Ivanhoe Perelson and Jyl Freed, friends who gave countless hours of proofreading, tear wiping and endless support; Jim and Georgia Donovan, friends and motivators who kept me moving in the right direction; and to my daughters, Alison and Sarah, who at times had less of me, so that animals could have more. Without you, I could not have done this.

My deep appreciation and special thanks are given to Kathy Hill, my dear friend and editor extraordinaire. Never squelching my voice, or the animals' messages, you have taken my words and made them suitable for the world. For this I am deeply indebted. Without your editing expertise, this book would never have come to be.

Finally, I thank my husband, Wayne, who has always been proud of who I am and what I do. Having taught me to have the courage of my convictions, you have shown me my dreams can become reality. Thank you for helping this dream come true.

Three Definitions

com-mu'-ni-cate v.   1) to pass along; transmit. 2) to make known; give or exchange information.   3) to be connected.[1]

te-lep'-a-thy n.   1). Parapsychology communication between minds by some means other than the normal sensory channels; transference of thought.[2]

an-thro-po-mor'-phism n.   1). an interpretation of what is not human or personal in terms of human or personal characteristics: Humanization.[3] 2). the attributing of human shape or characteristics to a god, animal, or inanimate thing.[4]

This book is about animal communication. It is not a book trying to establish the validity of *it's* existence, nor will it debate the question of anthropomorphism. It is written purely from the point of view that animals do indeed have feelings, emotions, life plans, and incredible wisdom to share with the world, if only humans will listen.

I have listened, as have others, and this book is a lasting, written record of what I have heard them say.

---

[1] Webster's New World Dictionary for Young Readers, New Revised Edition, Copyright 1989 by Simon & Schuster.

[2] Webster's New World™ College Dictionary, Third Edition, Copyright 1997 by Simon & Schuster, Inc.

[3] Webster's New Collegiate Dictionary, Copyright 1979 by G. & C. Merriam Company.

[4] Webster's New World™ College Dictionary, Third Edition, Copyright 1997 by Simon & Schuster, Inc.

Table of Contents

Introduction

All of my life I have shared my days with an animal by my side. Companion animals have brought more comfort and joy to my heart than probably any one person has in my lifetime. When I was a child, they were confidants to whom I entrusted my deepest secrets, furry tissues upon which I wiped my tears, and sounding boards for intriguing conversations I might get to have one day. They have been the deepest, most cherished, unforgettable beings that have ever entered my life, and I loved them all. I often wonder what my life would have been like without these sentient beings.

When I was a little girl, I believed that my Dad knew everything ～ a typical little girl's belief in her father. An avid outdoorsman, in love with wildlife, Dad always knew the name of every river or stream we passed on our weekend country drives. He dazzled me with all of the wildlife he would see in the fields we sped by, pointing out deer, rabbits and pheasants to us as we hurried to get a glimpse, each time we traveled on our three-hour trip to the Adirondack Mountains.

One day, on the way home from a weekend at camp, we stopped at a stranger's house. Eager to stretch my legs at this new place, I bounced along as we were led out back behind the house. Soon I was enamored with a wondrous sight: puppies, lots of little black-and-white-spotted Blue Tick Hound puppies. And we were going to choose one for our very own.

After much laughing and tumbling with pups, it was finally decided that one little male, whom I promptly named Blue, would be our new pet. Before leaving to bring our newest family member home, I stopped for one last look. I remember asking Dad, "What about the others? What about his mother? They'll really miss each other and he'll be really lonely."

I don't remember Dad's exact words given to me in reply, but he said pretty much this: "No, they won't. Blue will miss his family tonight, but his mother has just raised him on instinct. He won't remember her at all after a few days."

I looked at the rest of the puppies still playing happily with each other and wondered. Whether Dad was telling me this to quiet my concerns, or whether he really believed this to be true, two things I knew for sure: Blue would miss his mother and littermates much longer than that first night with us, and I no longer believed everything Daddy told me.

Thirteen years later, when Blue rode on my lap for the last time, on his final trip to the vet's, I agonized over what was about to transpire. For three days beforehand, we noticed Blue doing all of his favorite things, as if to experience those joys one last time. As tears fell, I recounted each one in my mind's eye. Blue was euthanized later that same day, and I came home with only his collar, and years of wonderful memories.

In time, my own spiritual beliefs comforted my grief. Life after death seemed confirmed, because for two years afterward, until I moved away, I would still hear Blue's bark, that unmistakable hound-dog howl, at 11 every night, the same time he had always been put out for that last potty run before bedtime. In the years since, I have often wondered how much easier it might have been for me had I been a communicator way back then.

I feel quite fortunate to be able to work every day with animals from near and far. I am still amazed at how my whole world reveals a deeper meaning when I can just sit lazily under a shade tree on a warm afternoon, with our three potbelly pigs flopped at my side. Because of this, it pleases me daily to see yet another human being open up to a whole new world they only dreamed existed ∼ the world their companion animal has just shared with them through me.

As they begin a new, more in-depth understanding of each other, I sit back and smile, confident that their boundaries of existence have just expanded exponentially, beyond time and space. Life is much more than I once ever believed it to be. Life truly is limitless. Accepting this as truth allows me and those I work with a greater determination to greet all of life with both a deep respect for all living creatures and an enthusiasm to learn more. Although I am still equally amazed at the gigantic hole left in my life when a companion animal is no longer there, these new horizons surpass that painful place we call death, lessening its sting and giving us strength to go on.

Because of all this, when I was first approached to do this book, I loved the idea but wasn't sure I had the writing abilities to do this tender subject justice. Four years working as an animal communicator for the public did leave my files dotted here and there with some of the more special conversations animals had shared with me ∼ many as they prepared for death, had just crossed over, or were in the process of doing so as we spoke.

What had always stood out most in my mind was the incredible wisdom and lack of fear the animals shared with me. When all was said and done, the connection broken, I carried forth with me the unconditional love those animals had for their people. Yet conveying the animals' messages with the same insight, wisdom and love just shared was very difficult, indeed. How, then, could I possibly write a book about it? I wasn't sure, but I knew that I had to try.

By the grace of God, the animals' direction, and an editor friend who helped give us all a properly written but uncensored voice, this book has come to fruition. These stories, quoted from the animals themselves, give tribute to not only their lives, but also to the incredible Spirit with which each being is endowed.

I hope you will come to believe, from these pages, that although a tremendous hole is left in our lives when our beloved animals cross over to the Rainbow Bridge, our heartbreak is really a testament to how much we truly loved them and does not need to signify an unending sorrow.

Communicating these animals' messages has given me some of the most beautiful experiences I have ever been allowed to share ∿ and I now share them with you, so you will know that their lives do go on.

I hope you will read this book time and again, each time finding new meaning in the messages within and perhaps a new understanding that all is well with the universe, even within the realm of what we call death.

The animals' views on this next stage of life have truly changed my life forever. I hope they can change yours, too.

Colleen Nicholson
Clay, New York
June 2000

The Rainbow Bridge

*Just this side of heaven is a place called Rainbow Bridge.
When beloved animals die here, they go to this lovely land. There
are meadows and hills for all of our special friends, so they can
run and play together. There is plenty of food, water and sunshine, and our friends are warm and comfortable.*

*All of the animals who had been ill or old are restored to
health and vigor. Those who were hurt or maimed are made
whole and strong again, just as we remember them in our dreams
of days and times gone by. The animals are happy and content,
except for one small thing; they each miss someone very special
to them, someone they had to leave behind.*

*They all run and play together, but the day comes when one
suddenly stops and looks into the distance. His bright eyes are
intent; His eager body begins to quiver. Suddenly he runs from
the group, flying over the green grass, his legs carrying him faster
and faster.*

*You have been spotted, and when you and your special friend
finally meet again, you cling together in joyous reunion.*

*Happy kisses rain upon your face. Your hands again caress
his beloved head. And, once more, you look into the trusting eyes
of your companion animal, so long gone from your life but never
absent from your heart.*

Then you cross the Rainbow Bridge, together…

—*Author Unknown*

Sometimes there's a request...

Chapter 1

Sheldon

"I'd like to make an appointment to speak with my dog, please.
I just lost him and I was told that you might be able to help."

A call coming in from California is not an unusual thing for me here
on the East Coast, but when this one arrived I hadn't been referred much
for help with lost animals. Tina was very upset, so in order to help her
quickly find her little Sheltie dog, Sheldon, I slipped her into the emergency slot that I always keep open in my daily schedule for situations
that just can't wait.

An hour later, as I prepared myself for her call, I sat at my desk
trying to tune into Sheldon and where he might be. Immediately he was
there and eager to communicate, although I was having difficulty inter-
preting his message ⁓ or so I thought. Before Tina's call even rang
through, I began writing down the information I was receiving. Right
away I got the impression that he was just fine. This was a relief.

The next impressions Sheldon shared were pictures of a big, bright,
open place, that was pretty devoid of definition, along with the feeling of
not wanting to come back home.

"Oh *great*," I muttered to myself. "How in the world am I going to
tell this woman that her lost dog doesn't want to come back?"

I wondered. Had Sheldon been an abused dog who had finally
made his escape, but now a guilty, grieving human wanted a second
chance? This scenario didn't really seem right to me, because Tina had
seemed very sincere about speaking to her lost dog. But then I was all

3

the way across the country. Maybe I was missing something very important in the few moments of conversation we had spent as I booked her appointment? When the phone rang, right on time, I put down my pen, took a deep breath and answered.

It was obvious she had been crying. I wasn't sure how I was going to help soothe Tina's grief with the news I had to share, but in my mind's eye Sheldon was looking right at me, anxiously waiting for me to tell his "mom" what he was conveying. A pretty faithful companion for a dog who may have been abused, I thought.

Another deep breath, then I began to tell Tina what Sheldon had just shared with me. I started by letting her know that he seemed to be just fine. I described the vagueness of the place I was shown, where he apparently now was. Then I dug in and told her that I didn't know how to say it, but that Sheldon didn't really want to come back. Those few seconds of silence, as Tina sniffed and blew her nose, seemed like an eternity. I had no idea what to expect when the conversation resumed, so I sat frozen, waiting for her response.

"I'm not surprised," she said slowly as she sniffed once more and quietly regained her composure.

Now my head was reeling. What happened? Cautiously, I continued, "Tina, I can't really tell where Sheldon is because I can't see anything that might be recognizable to you. I'm sorry, but I'm afraid that I can't help you."

"Oh, yes … you are helping. I know exactly where he is," Tina said with a deep sigh.

"You do?" I asked, amazed at how she could know this when I hadn't told her much of anything about Sheldon's surroundings.

"So you can go get him now? Did you lose him close to home?"

I was thinking to myself how easy this was. The "free spirit" stereotype Eastern folks have of Californians playfully flickered through my mind, and I decided this had to be why Tina could figure out Sheldon's whereabouts and I couldn't. The brief reprieve from seriousness was welcome but didn't last very long. Tina cleared her voice and began to speak again.

"Oh, I can't go get him," she said, in a patient voice, a voice that questioned my sanity. "I lost him a few days ago."

Not knowing what to think at this point, I sat there dumbfounded. Apparently realizing the state I was in, Tina softly added, "My Sheldon died on Wednesday."

Now *this* was embarrassing. It had never entered my mind that Sheldon had crossed over the Rainbow Bridge. When Tina first said she had lost her dog, I had taken it literally.

With a fully flushed face, I responded with relief, "Oh, I'm sorry, Tina! I thought he was lost in the neighborhood. That explains why he doesn't really want to come home."

Tina agreed.

I am an Animal Communicator. I am not psychic. There is a big difference in my mind. Animal communication is a form of telepathy we can utilize to communicate with the animals around us. It is my deepest belief that we *all* are capable of this, but most of us have simply forgotten how. Anyone who has ever loved an animal truly has communicated with them. Most often it is passed off as reading body language or just recognizing a routine in an animal's life. This may be true to some extent, but that inner knowing a caregiver gets when they look at their beloved companion and just know that something is wrong, is communicating with them on a level beyond the physical. Most likely, it just never had a name before.

Universal Language is the highest language with which we can communicate. People may refer to it as innate wisdom, inner truth or instinct. Many pigs and horses I've spoken with have called it "the Knowing."

When accessing Universal Language, individual languages are not a barrier, or even a consideration, because it consists of images, emotions, physical sensations and blocks of thought. So when animals communicate their Knowing to me, they do so using one or more of these forms. My job then, is to interpret it all, and then to convey their message to others in everyday language.

Every time we form a thought, a mental image, or picture, is formed in our mind. Through my work with animals, I have come to believe that this is the most important form of communication, not only as they use it with each other, but also as they communicate across species.

The pictures I commonly see are soft and subtle, but they can contain very specific images. Usually they appear to be what the animal is either doing or wants to do, or a picture of whom they are referring to. I simply interpret the pictures and relay their content, adding in any feelings or sensations that may be accompanying them.

When animals share feelings, I can feel them in my own body. If an animal is grieving, I feel their grief, and many times tears will run down my cheeks even though I'm not the one who is sad.

When an animal is ill, often the biggest fear that those around them face comes from the belief that their beloved pet cannot speak to tell them what is wrong. If they are sick or in pain, often they'll share with me what hurts them and where. In my own body, I can then feel their area of discomfort, making this form of communication a wonderful tool when it comes to health care. Time after time I have had confirmation from clients who followed up a health-related communication with a visit to their veterinarian. When the area their animal had identified as the problem spot was checked by the vet, the problem was found! This is most rewarding, indeed, especially for the animal.

The melding of these forms of communication actually creates another. More complex and a bit harder to explain, "blocks of thought" consist of a *lot* of information. As I begin to decipher the pictures, the colours, sensations, emotions and feelings, the animals will usually pay careful attention to my interpretive processes, to ensure I am communicating their thoughts accurately. If I start stumbling around for descriptive words to use, they will often stop me before I get a sentence finished, only to start me again in a new direction. It is within this sphere of specificity that auditory "words" most often come, so considering that I've already said animal communication is in the realm of Universal Language ∼ beyond cultural differences ∼ this point needs clarification.

I do not really *hear* the animals speak the words, but my voice will seem to mimic what I'm hearing as it takes on different tones, inflections and syntax that are not normal to the way I speak. It's as if I am remembering the way a friend sounds when they speak. Some animals have a deep voice, others whisper, some speak with a commanding tone, and others are meek and mild. Most intriguing to me is when they seem to flip through my vocabulary in an effort to find the right word for me to use, best conveying what they wish to communicate. This *always* turns out to be a word I would never think to use. And I am sure that in their flipping they've been pretty disappointed with my limited vocabulary. In an effort to often appease them all, I've bought a thesaurus.

A typical conversation with an animal uses all these forms of communication, and the best communications often come when I am receiving information so fast that I speak it before thinking. These messages almost always relate to things that I couldn't have known, and are then confirmed by the astonished people I'm communicating for. For this reason, I try to keep my logical mind out of the process, so as not to form opinions that might interfere with a message's content as it filters through my belief system, or to limit its entirety by imposing my thoughts on the subject, carrying me off in a direction of my own. To best accomplish this, I ask for very limited information beforehand.

Probably the most difficult aspect of any animal communication is taking the incredible amount of information usually given to me from the vast viewpoint one is in when working within Universal Language, and transferring it all down into the minuscule, and often pathetic, translation of human language. It's like trying to fit a real-life ocean liner into a little soda bottle!

So what do animals like to talk about? Anything and everything! Some animals are better communicators than others, just like some people are better speakers or storytellers than others. Some animals have a great sense of humour and enjoy good-hearted mischief, taking pride in their ability to "get your goat," so to speak. Others like to offer their wisdom and philosophies on life, death and other noble topics, as they see them pertaining to themselves, their species, their human caregivers, or other companions. One thing for sure is that animals aren't used to having humans truly listen. Once they realize we are listening, they usually have much to say.

They also like to discuss their health and diet, their likes and dislikes, sometimes where behavior problems are stemming from, and on into their own beautiful views on life.

You will find my most treasured conversations in this book, because they are the ones that have dealt with death and dying. This is because animals do not view death as we humans do. For them it's just another step upon a long journey of experiences. They almost always embrace the next step with a sense of adventure, looking forward to moving on.

The only time this is not conveyed to me is when they believe their families are desperately clinging onto them and the hope of just one more day with their faithful friend. In our own grief and fear, many times we cause them added suffering, which they need not endure if we could just let go, as hard as that may be to us.

As you read this book, I hope you will come to realize our animal friends are not gone forever, they are just transformed into a greater being, one of brilliance, without pain, suffering or physical constraints.

Many times, too, this transcended being is one whom we will meet again, when it is our time to cross over to the other side of life. I've been changed forever by the pictures, feelings and words the animals have shared with me for their families left behind. I hope they will change your life, too.

In a common thread among the various books about near-death experiences, authors often talk about having received a wonderful, prophetic message from a glorious being of light and love, whom they met during the time their body was clinically dead. Animals who are near death, or those who have recently crossed over, often speak of ethereal beings too, who have greeted them or tended to them for a while. Their message is always uplifting, one of how life goes on after the physical body is shed.

Animals have taught me that our life-force and experiences do not end with the passing of a mere body, but that they simply travel on into a different form of "being." I view this as Soul going home ⁓ to the place from which we all first came.

I have found these messages very soothing to grieving human companions, as they give hope to survivors, transforming some of their grief into little smiles and replacing some of their tears with joyful memories of the life and love they shared with their beloved animal.

That is what this book is all about, the messages and stories of companion animals as they approach death, or as Soul awakens in heaven. I've no doubt that while these animal communications have transcended the physical boundaries of both time and space, their message will span the ages.

Back to my story about Tina and Sheldon … As the conversation went on, Sheldon began to explain to Tina that she shouldn't worry about him. He was just fine and waiting for her to come, too. Shocked at the statement that had just flown out of my mouth, I reeled back. This was a message that I did not feel comfortable sharing. I am not a fortune teller, and I did not want to sound like one. This time Tina quickly sensed the awkward place I was in, again, and jumped in to save me from fumbling around for words.

"That's okay, Colleen, He's right! I've had a heart transplant and I know that it won't last forever. Sheldon stayed with me through all of that, and I miss him so much now. I know he will wait for me. He was the best friend ever."

At the time of our conversation, almost a week had passed since Sheldon's crossing, and Tina wanted to close it with any last thoughts he had to share. I don't recall much more of what we spoke about that day, but one last thing that stands out in my mind is Sheldon's mention of a red ball. Tina couldn't place it, as Sheldon only had a blue ball, which he loved. But Sheldon was insistent that he liked the red ball. He wanted to keep it with him.

Our conversation ended with Sheldon confirming that he would indeed be there the following Sunday, when friends and family were to gather at a party in his honour. His ashes were to be buried under the lilac tree, where he had loved to sleep. He truly was a beloved dog.

A week later, Tina called back. She told me the memorial party had been a wonderful event, with many friends and family there to honour Sheldon and laugh at the many funny memories he had left them with. They even raised their wine glasses in a special toast just for him.

For days before, the red ball he'd mentioned haunted Tina, because he wanted it buried with his ashes. She searched the house for it, to no avail. When Sunday arrived and no red ball had been found, she put his favorite old blue ball into his grave and blew kisses to her heavenly friend. To her surprise, friends and family stepped forward, tossing in miniature red carnations she had bought for him.

"You know, when everyone was done and I looked down in there, there must have been a dozen or more red flowers ∽ and they looked just like red balls to me." ✧

Vincent

*"Give me your okay to go.
I don't want to leave you 'til then."*

It is very hard for me when I have a call come in from someone who is devastated over their companion animal's crossing. Of course, we all are really sad when losing a friend, but when I can hear the sobs in their voice and know tears fill their eyes, it's sometimes difficult for me to concentrate while at the same time being sympathetic to their grief. I know how they feel, I've been there myself. When Maxine called her grief had been hanging on for weeks. But although sobs were in her voice, and I'm sure tears filled her eyes, Vincent spoke loudly and clearly, distracting me from both her emotions and my own.

"I've lost my Vincent," she said, pausing to compose herself before going on. "I called him, Vincent V.I.P., for Very Important Pig."

Vincent had died suddenly a few weeks before, and Maxine's friend had recommended she call me because she was having such a difficult time. They both hoped I could help Maxine deal with this huge loss, while helping Vincent's companion, Elliott, deal with his grief as well. After all, pigs are herd animals, and now Elliott had lost both his friend and his herd.

We talked for a short time and the conversation flowed back and forth easily. Vincent seemed a very sweet, loving, and soft pig. He spoke tenderly to me and showed me pictures of everything he was trying to convey. He began to speak about a special can and how Maxine should put some mementos into it. I wasn't sure what he was explaining to me as he showed me something that looked like a coffee can. I wondered outloud if perhaps he'd had a favorite one that he would drag out from the lower kitchen cabinets. Maxine, however, knew just what Vincent was referring to because after he'd died, she'd had his remains cremated. They had arrived in a can just like he described ∼ nothing fancy, just a plain ol' can.

Eventually, Vincent quieted, directing me to speak with Elliott. He was most concerned about his friend, and he wanted Elliott to know that he was not really that far away.

Elliott shyly shared his deep grief with me, an aching that came from the very bottom of his heart. I found it was harder for me to deal with his grief than Maxine's. The most encouraging part was that he was willing to communicate with me, I felt this was a big step for him to make toward recovery.

He showed me how he slept alone now, and that night time was the loneliest for him. During the day, he showed me himself grazing all alone, and just him lying in a strip of sunlight, which they used to nap together in. He missed Vincent very much, and I believe Elliott's grief was worse because he'd been with Vincent ever since he had come to live there. He'd also been with Vincent when he collapsed.

Elliott pictured how he wanted to spend more time on his mom's lap, but he wasn't sure he was brave enough to do so. He did find comfort in being near her more, but it wasn't the same as being with Vincent. Maxine understood. As I spoke with Elliott, I tried to explain to him that if he listened carefully, he would hear Vincent still. Perhaps that would help him feel better about his friend? Elliott didn't know, but he thought he would go think about that for a while.

Vincent waited patiently for me to finish speaking with Elliott, then went on to explain to his mom that something had ruptured inside of him, that it was nothing she had done.

He told me he'd had a small, round lump, which he was born with, but recently it had begun to get bigger. He showed me a picture of the location of the lump, and it seemed to be a space between the upper and lower sinus passages, inside the middle of his head, near the entryway into his throat. Although we'll never know for sure if this was really the root of his problem, Maxine was thankful for the information and confirmed that this could well have been what happened to Vincent because it correlated with some of the ideas his vet had shared with her.

Vincent apologized about the mess that she had found when his lump had ruptured suddenly. He did not want her to remember this whenever she thought of him, and then he began a message that touched us both deeply, a memento she later put into Vincent's can.

> *"I worry about you all, Mom, and my friend Elliott is still crying. I'm a good pig and I want to go on here ⁓ to the place I'll stay before going back there. But I don't want to go until you are happy. So get happy soon, so I can leave you with a smile.*
>
> *"I have no pain or sadness, just a soft, warm fog that I keep seeing everyone there in. This (picture) I will take with me. These things stay with a pig, you know.*
>
> *"Give me your okay to go. I don't want to leave you 'til then. I know you can do it because Elliott will help you. He needs your special V.I.P. treatment.*
>
> *"My most favorite thing you did for me was to pet me, from my eyes to behind my ears, whenever you looked at me really close.*
>
> *"Will you put a picture of me by Elliott's bed, please? And will you give him something of mine that isn't washed? He will need another pig, because Elliott needs two.*
>
> *"Tell Elliott all about me, because when I tell him, he doesn't hear me. He will hear me again, if you tell him to listen, because I will always be on the winds of my herd's Knowing.*
>
> *"Maybe you will put a picture of me and Elliott by my can? Then, someday when Elliott comes here, you can put him in my can, too.*
>
> *"You will hear me laugh again, Mom. You will al-*

ways hear me on the wind, like Elliott, and sometimes the wind will be soft ∼ like me."

I left the conversation knowing that the grief Maxine and Elliott shared was a deep one that only time would heal. I also left knowing what Vincent was willing to wait around until Maxine could learn to smile when she thought of him, instead of bursting into tears. For me, it was a kind of proof that deep grief can hold loved ones nearby, when in fact they are ready to move on. And although Vincent said he did have plans to move on, it would only be when Maxine was really ready to let him go. Whenever that was to be, I felt sure they would be together again, one day.

It was a special conversation for me too, because I learned that a relationship doesn't necessarily end when death comes knocking at the door. When we give love, and it is returned unconditionally, a special bond is forged. Then, when the door opens and we take our last breath, we can step through it with confidence, as we move onward toward the Rainbow Bridge ∼ where animals and their loved ones wait for each other ∼ in heaven. ✿

Sometimes there's

       confirmation...

Chapter 2

Squirrel

"Does she like to be up high, Eleni? She's showing me pictures of being way up high. I think she is walking on the roof!"

This was my first introduction to Eleni and her little companion cat, and it was surprising, at least. Although I'd known how cats often do like to perch up high, this was quite beyond the height of your typical cat tree or refrigerator. With Squirrel, there was a sense of elation from great heights, and she was not doing it just so she could look down upon those beneath her.

"Oh yes, that would be her!" Eleni gasped with amazement. Her first time communicating with an animal was off to an exciting start.

Squirrel had been named appropriately. A soft gray cat boasting a touch of black and a lighter coloured belly, she did resemble a squirrel. But more than her resemblance through colouring, Squirrel really acted like one.

Eleni quickly told me how her cat loved to be way up high, describing some of the daredevil antics she'd been known to do at great heights. After we both had a few good laughs, Eleni refocused on why she had wanted to have this communication with Squirrel and began by asking her if she wanted to speak first.

Squirrel had lots to say, and it came without hesitation. After listening intently to all she wanted to share, Eleni asked Squirrel a lot of the same questions I usually hear asked during a first communication. The entire time Squirrel gave us her undivided attention, answering each question thoughtfully.

During this time, I came to learn how Squirrel had been quite ill only a short time before. With a diagnosis of kidney disease, the outlook for Squirrel had been grave. But after she was released from the veterinary hospital, Eleni used natural therapies to help nurse her failing friend back to health. Squirrel had recovered well, and with her vitality quite intact. Satisfied that she had asked Squirrel every question on her list, Eleni finished their communication and we all parted happily.

Some months later, I spoke with Squirrel again, about five days after her death. She was 19 years old when she crossed over in her sleep, the result of kidney failure. Through sobs, Eleni described how Squirrel had been her old self again, up until her kidneys began to fail one month before her passing.

Unable to euthanize her beloved companion as others suggested, she explained how she couldn't bear the thought, even though natural therapies weren't working as they had before. Anguished, she'd held on, and Squirrel's health declined steadily, day by day. In the days that followed Squirrel's death, Eleni was haunted by the fear she'd been too selfish, causing her friend undue pain and suffering. However, Squirrel had no resentments.

I was surprised it had taken a whole month for Squirrel's body to finally give out once her kidneys began to fail again, but before I had the opportunity to ponder this thought, Squirrel spoke right up. Sounding as lively as the first time we'd met, she plainly informed me that she was "in for the long haul." And, when her mom just couldn't let her go, it had become her job to take care of Eleni.

"I just didn't pay any attention to my body. It didn't hurt as much that way," Squirrel briefly explained. This was a comfort to Eleni's aching heart.

Squirrel's explanation was not a new idea to me. It's a phenomenon I have experienced with a lot of animals who are either dying or suffering from a debilitating illness. It appears they have an ability to willingly leave their body, perhaps entering a different mental sphere where pain does not exist. It's not the same as leaving the body upon death, because these animals still seem to be connected somehow, and most often their humans note that they're sleeping much more than usual.

True to my previous experiences, I learned that Squirrel followed this same pattern until a few days before she passed over. When her ability to ignore the pain and discomfort dissolved, Squirrel conveyed that she simply chose a moment, then left. As devastated as Eleni was, I was confident Squirrel believed her mom could handle the separation. And though physically gone, as I suspected, she didn't really go far.

"I was in a hurry to get back to the trees!" Vitality flowed from Squirrel's words, spoken from one still quite agile and alive.

Today, when I close my eyes, I can still see her gray body flying through the treetops, jumping from limb to limb, then leaping to a rooftop below.

Eleni now shares her life with two other companion cats, each special in their own right, perhaps each equally destined to become as legendary to her as Squirrel.

At times, her heart still aches for Squirrel, but when she finds herself melancholy over her friend's physical absence, she wanders to the window to gaze out back at the perfect memorial she'd found for Squirrel. Beckoning with many wonderful memories as it sits there beneath the trees, the antiqued gray squirrel marks the place Squirrel's body was buried. The marker among the trees ∼ a fitting monument for this friend, moved on.

On a warm summer day the following year, in a serene cottage setting, a group gathered for an introductory seminar designed to help participants open new lines of communication with animals. Eleni was in attendance.

We started by using animals I've worked with often, knowing they have always been good communicators for me. After each participant chose a picture of the animal they felt drawn to communicate with, I guided them through the first simple steps I often use. My goal was not only to teach them a process, but also to be able to confirm their experiences.

As the first exercise ended and the class members shared their experiences, intrigue turned to laughter and huge smiles. With their first success achieved, we moved on to the second exercise, with each person chosing an animal of another participant's.

I noticed Eleni's fingers gripping her old picture of Squirrel. I cautioned everyone to share only basic information, giving less opportunity for an experience to be coloured by preconceived ideas.

From across the room, a short time later, I saw a few tears roll down Eleni's smiling face as Janice shared the experience she'd just had with Squirrel. As I walked over to join them, Janice described how easy Squirrel had been to communicate with, but she was confused by something odd that she had felt, something she was sure meant her communication had not been a very clear one.

"She shared with me what it feels like to jump through tree branches, high up in the air. She said she had been a squirrel in another lifetime!" Janice shrugged her shoulders as she pondered Squirrel's picture. Her voice half stated the remark, while questioning it at the same time.

I thought back to the first impressions I had enjoyed with Squirrel during our first conversation. I knew how Janice felt.

Eleni, on the other hand, beamed with joy, all the while nodding her head yes, to confirm Janice's experience.

"Oh, that's my Squirrel, alright," she said, proudly wiping the tears from her face. "She loved to be up as high as she could go."

Eleni began to tell Janice more about her cat, so Janice would understand just how in tune with Squirrel she had truly been. As the two huddled together over the well-worn picture of this beloved cat, I began to move my attention to a horse experience going on behind me. Boo-Boo the thoroughbred had made contact, too.

As I walked away, Janice was reading to Eleni from the notes she'd scribbled during her communication with Squirrel. A simple message full of meaning, it was a fitting end-note for me, and I listened with a full heart, knowing that yet another connection had been made.

"Being a cat was okay, but I really liked that squirrel body."

Then Janice's voice trailed off, getting lost in the background conversations.

Sometimes there's a lesson...

Chapter 3

Tissy's Legacy

"Our mother taught us about life, and purpose, and how to be a good pig. She is now on the winds of my herd's Knowing." Penny

Walls of windows enveloped me as I sat on the sofa in my bridesmaid dress, in the sunroom of Kathleen's ranch. The setting winter sun had just broken through the clouds, casting a beautiful glow on the wet trees and fields, lending a feeling of peacefulness that twilight was about to descend upon us.

Gazing across the yard toward the "pig park," I fondly thought about Tissy, one of Kathleen's potbellied pigs, and how her death seemed to have left a big hole, both in her herd and in my heart. She'd had a big impact upon my life when she was here, and I wondered if that was the reason I felt so saddened by her crossing. My eyes began to fill with tears, and I reached to wipe one away.

Penny, one of Tissy's grown piglets, suddenly spoke loudly, clearly, and without a hint of sadness. I paused for a moment, then reached for a pen and wrote her brief message down on a scrap of paper. As I laid the pen to rest a smile erupted, and wonderful memories came flooding back.

Pondering whether there is a purpose to our lives has given scholars and theologians something to think about for eons. For us to extend this same belief to animals is most likely rare, if thought about at all, yet this story proves differently. This story is about a spoken letter of life and purpose, composed and entrusted to me by Tissy, a forthright and can-

23

did potbelly sow, as decisions were being made about where her littlest piglet would spend her life. I always take great interest when an animal allows me to listen in, but this message was even more special because this little piglet came to live with me.

Happily, I now take you back to the beginning of Tissy's story, a pig's legacy, and how the "purpose of life" touches all living beings.

The Beginning:

Thrilled to be back visiting my favorite Texas herd, I no sooner had arrived than I hoiked my trotters to the pig park, named appropriately by Sadie, the first and oldest pig on the ranch. For Kathleen, it was time for evening chores. For me, it was time to mingle with a herd I had long missed. Stopping to speak with each pig I came upon, I rambled on and on about how pleased I was to see them again. I wasn't surprised though to be met with limited enthusiasm ∼ you see, it was their dinnertime ... they are pigs ... need I say more?

If you've never borne witness to pigs at mealtime, you're really missing out. Not only do they squeal with anticipation over a delicious meal, no matter what food you feed, they also smack their lips, look for more and truly enjoy every morsel you share. If a pig doesn't come running at mealtime, there is something wrong.

Happy to remember many of the pigs' names, I considered this no small feat in a herd of 50-some pigs. Amid snorts and grunts, they gathered around me for an extra handout, and I laughed as I watched the "pot" bellies of various sizes sway to and fro, as they hurried from one spot to the next.

Sweetie, a big black barrow, banged me in the knee, asking for another treat from the stash he knew I had stuffed in my pockets. Reaching down to deposit one into his waiting and open mouth, I thought about how Sweetie had been left here by his family for boarding one day, and then never picked up. Even though they still sent board money for his care every month, it had been years since they'd come to see him.

When I first met Sweetie, he was quite the bully, and therefore elicited anger from many. He told me plainly that this was "his herd," and he did not want to be viewed as an outsider. Kathleen had said that from that moment on she told Sweetie he was hers and that he was here to stay, and that ever since he has been a changed pig. He isn't a big bully anymore, even though he still can thump a knee hard when he feels you aren't doling out treats fast enough for his pleasure.

Soon, Ruth ran by on her way to a water bowl, anxious to get a drink and to cool down on this hot day. Very special to Kathleen, Ruth was the only piglet born into a litter that came during a hard time in her life, as her mother-in-law was dying. She always felt Ruth was mystical, special, and it was reflected in the name she gave her. Like so many of the pigs here in the pig park, Ruth was yet another Kathleen said would never leave the ranch.

I wandered on, calling all the names I remembered. Abby, Chrissy Pig, Charlotte, Lulu, and Mary were just some of my pig friends who stopped to say hello, remembering me as I did them. I had special pats for the new pigs too, who flew by during the dinnertime waltz. I was in pig heaven, and Kathleen was doing all of the work.

After the pools and water bowls were filled for the night, Kathleen and I attended to Tina, a little pig who had recently become lame in her front legs. Unable to walk or fend for herself, she was being picked on by some of the herd, so we readied the last free pen to put Tina into. Here she could be observed and tended to, without worry of her being trampled or injured further in a mealtime rush.

Gretel was having some trouble with her autumn allergies, while her aunt, Martha, had begun to tip her head to the side, indicating that an ear infection was ailing her. So they joined Tina in her new private pen adjacent to the pig park. Barely removed from the main herd, now all three girls could be medicated and doted on more easily.

By now, the others were realizing there were simply no crumbs left to be found. Many of them headed for their favorite sleeping places as we headed for the gate, passing the few diehards who still searched the park's feeding area in vain. Tissy, conceding that her dinner was indeed over, passed us by on her way to the barn. As she did so, Kathleen wondered aloud, "I wonder when Tissy will have her babies?"

"Four or five days," came an unexpectedly prompt and matter-of-fact reply, as Tissy hurried by me in search of the best spot to sleep for the night. Noticing how her portly belly almost touched the ground, I sighed a sympathetic sigh. I knew that feeling, but I was unaware I had spoken her response outloud.

"Four or five days?" Kathleen's startled comment snapped me back to my senses as I realized what had just happened. Neither of us expected an answer to a question merely muttered in tired curiosity.

"I wonder where I'll put her now that Tina and the girls are in the nursery pen," she said.

Without so much as a slowed step or turn of an ear, the reply came rocketing back, "How about on the porch?"

Stopping in our tracks, we both turned toward Tissy, who was now halfway to the barn.

"On the porch?" I asked in amazement. "Where the heck is the porch?"

Tissy's tail had now cleared the doorway and she disappeared into the barn. Inside, squeals and other disgruntled sounds were heard as each pig discussed, rather loudly, the proposed sleeping arrangements for the night. I, on the other hoof, remained motionless, surely my eyes twinkling with joy as I dismissed the possibility that I could have made this up.

Turning to Kathleen, I watched as she looked to the back of the barn, as if contemplating a how-to approach.

"Well," she sighed, "that is Tissy's favorite place to lie in the morning. But I don't know how I can contain the piglets while keeping the others out."

"What do you mean? You've got a porch back there?" I blurted out in doubt. Surely I must have missed something. "Are you kidding me, Kathleen?"

"No," she said plainly. "You won't believe this but behind the barn there, where we just were, well that's the porch, and Tissy, along with a few others, like Sadie and Charlotte, likes to take naps there every morning after breakfast."

I looked toward the back of the barn as I started walking that way. My New England upbringing had taught me that a "porch" was a beautiful extension for outdoor living, attached to the front of a two-story, shuttered home, with lattice work underneath it where cottage wild-flowers grew. I was positive I hadn't seen such a structure in the pig park, and sure enough, I arrived to find nothing of the sort. It seems that in Texas, a barn porch can be as simple as a four-inch raised platform with a roof overhead. It's just enough to keep thing out of the elements. This was the porch of Tissy's nursery dreams, and I stood in disbelief.

Kathleen laughed at me for a long time. As she chuckled, she moved some things around in a halfhearted attempt to decide if a suitable nursery could be fashioned there for Tissy and her soon-to-be litter.

"I don't think this will do," she mused, before turning to me and chuckling once more. "Besides, I don't think Tissy is due for a couple weeks yet. Tina will probably be better by then and that pen will be free for her to use."

Brushing off her hands and wiping perspiration from her brow, Kathleen stood and looked out over the pasture toward the cattle that were headed back from the woods for the night. Even though the sun was setting, it was still quite warm, and slowly we headed for the house.

I marveled at how quiet it had suddenly become, no doubt because the pigs were finally all settled in for the night. Silently, I whispered goodnight to Ethel and Ransom, and the other pigs who had private quarters along the side of the pig park, like Tina. Kathleen, however, had other things on her mind, and soon the peaceful moment was broken as she slowed her pace, then queried, "I wonder how many she'll have?"

"Two boars, a sow and a gilt," Tissy retorted, although she was presumed to be tucked into the straw inside the barn, fast asleep for the night, with her herd piled up along side her. It was beyond doubt now ∼ Tissy was indeed orchestrating this conversation, and I was just a bystander who happened to be able to hear it.

Five days later, I packed my bags, said good-bye to each pig, and kissed as many snooties as possible before climbing into Kathleen's van. A wonderful visit was drawing to a close.

All the way to the airport, we talked and laughed about many of the things we had done and discussed that week. Of course, Tissy was part of our conversation. Kathleen dropped me at the airport's check-in gate, and I wrestled with my luggage while she headed back home.

Once I was on board, a few tears slid down my cheeks as the plane's jet engines began to roar for takeoff. As the ground slipped away from underneath me, I wiped my face dry and began to think of my own family and herd who waited for me at home. Surely I was missed, and I began to look forward to the "Welcome Home" hugs and kisses I would be receiving in a few short hours.

The day-in-and-day-out routine of pet pigs is something they strive to live by. I think it's one of those unwritten "universal laws" that shouldn't be messed with, because when a pig's schedule is interrupted there usually is hell to pay. My leaving for Texas had certainly put a crimp into Clover's and Harry's lifestyle for a few days, and I was about to find out just how long a pig can hold a grudge.

Hurrying through the door, ready to lavish the boys with my undying affection, I was met with such cold shoulders that my jaw dropped in despair. It was as if I were invisible, although my suitcase did bear a good rooting through.

The next morning, Kathleen called early. "You won't believe it," she said, sounding half excited and half exhausted at the same time. "When I got home from the airport and went to feed the pigs, I noticed Tissy didn't come out to eat. I went to look for her afterward, and oh, you'll love this: I found her on the porch, in labour. She was just lying there, huffing and puffing. She hadn't even made a nest. That's unheard of for her."

"'Well, I bet you'd like some straw,' I told her. And when I brought it out, she got up and fixed a nice nest."

"Are you kidding me?" I exclaimed in a voice loud enough to make everyone around me stop what they were doing to look my way. "So she had her piglets? Right on the day she said she would?"

"It gets better, Colleen. Guess what she had?"

"Was it the right number? Did she have four?" I asked.

The pause in her voice seemed very long before Kathleen replied, "Two boars, a sow and a gilt. And she had one stillborn boar, too."

I felt I should have played the lottery that day. No way could I have known all of this if Tissy hadn't told me.

Unbelievable. The ramifications of it all began to fill my head. What if animals could readily tell you this kind of information? How easy it would be to prepare for babies you knew would be born on a certain day. Knowing how many of each sex was expected was even better. But in the middle of my mind-blowing process, I suddenly did the math and realized that Tissy had told us she'd have four piglets.

"Wait, she had five," I said, as I began to rationalize this in my mind. "If she knew so much about when and where she would have these babies, why would she make a mistake with the number? Do you think she didn't count the third boar because he was stillborn, Kath?"

"Hmm, that makes sense. He wasn't fully formed and it looked like he stopped growing a month ago. I've seen that before," she said.

Although feeling a bit sad about the stillborn piglet, I couldn't help but be overwhelmed with excitement over everything else.

"Well this is too wonderful for words. I just can't believe it," I said. "Congratulations to Tissy and the whole herd. I can't wait for pictures."

Our conversation ended and I went off to tell my family the incredible Texas news. "Why is it I always seem to leave a day too soon? If I'd stayed one more day, I would've been there when they were born. How great would that have been?"

My husband, Wayne, was very impressed with the whole story, imagining himself what this could mean in the bigger picture of life. Sarah and Alison, my daughters, found the story amusing, however I knew Sarah, at 17, quietly worried that her mother was losing a grip in the real world, as evidenced by my excitement level over this whole thing. Clover and Harry pretended not to hear a word of it, still making me pay for having disrupted their lives the week before. I went in search of a "Congratulations" card.

A day later, Kathleen sent word that one of the two boys had died soon after we'd spoken. She told me in her note that there must have been something wrong with him, too, as he never nursed well and wouldn't take a bottle. But the other three were doing great.

She described the hay house she had built them, securing a heat lamp to the top where it could keep the piglets warm but not be in danger of causing a fire. She also went on to describe how this was the first litter she'd ever raised right in the main herd.

"Tissy's a good mom, though," she wrote. "She lets the others get close enough to see, but they don't test her resolve to keep them safe. The piglets run around and can get under the fencing in places. But they're so cute, especially the littlest one. Remember how tiny Gretel was? Well, this little one is just a tiny bit bigger."

I did remember Gretel's piglet pictures. In fact, she was always one of my favorite pigs to listen to because of her great song-writing abilities. I smiled as I wondered if any of these new pigs would like to sing too; after all, they were full siblings. True to form, it wasn't long before Gretel had composed a new song. It began, "Ohhhh, I love it when there's babies on the farm."

The Middle:

Four months later, I returned to Texas to work, play, and of course to greet Tissy, who sported a new, more slender figure, and her three weaned babies.

The little boy was so cute. Now a barrow (a neutered boar), this little polka-dotted guy was in a quarantine pen while he waited to move to his new home in Venezuela. A wealthy family there anxiously awaited the arrival of their new, soon-to-be-cherished pet pig.

Iris was in a pen by herself, learning socializing skills with humans. Kathleen was taking her to a potbelly pig show in San Antonio later that week, so harness training was needed, too. Her beautiful conformation made her good potential as a breeding sow when she grew older, although now she was considered a gilt, which is a young female.

The littlest piglet lived in the main herd, and she was still tiny alright. Since she did not yet have a name, I called her "Baby." However it didn't matter if I called her at all. Whenever I was sitting on the ground, or crouched to dote on another pig, she would come to nip at my coat or pant legs, asking for the attention she was too shy to stay and enjoy. By the third day though, she let me scratch her good. Uncontrollably, she suddenly tipped over onto the ground.

"Oh no! I think I'm broken," she exclaimed in a voice as small as she was. This was obviously her first experience in the paralysing ecstasy a good belly rub will produce. Laughing out loud, I startled her. She struggled to regain her footing, then darted back off to safety in the middle of the herd.

Little did I know then that this little pig would one day be mine, but to this day I can still hear her first little words whenever I tip a pig for a good belly rub. Unfortunately for them, to this day I still often startle them when I laugh out loud, delighted with my well-honed "pig-tipping" powers.

The Message:

A few months later, while contemplating all I needed to do to prepare for this little pig's arrival, my mind went back to the first time I met her, then back further to when I first learned from Tissy that she was accounted for, even before her birth. Astounded by my great fortune to have been a part of something so magnificent, I closed my eyes and wondered how sad it would be for this little pig to travel so far from home. In that moment, I almost felt guilty for bringing her here, but a story began to unfold before me and I soon realized it was Tissy speaking to her baby, so I reached for my pen and began to write what I heard.

> "It is very important for babies from our farm to go into the world with special talents and goodness. They do not have to sing or hum, but need to be happy pigs that make their new herd smile. When my babies go away I talk to them, and tell them how special they are, and they will always hear me talk to them when they are far away.
>
> "Sadie says that your original herd is the herd you come back to when time is no more and the next world hasn't opened its doors to you. It is a brief, breezy visit but long enough to touch the love of those from which you came, those from where you originated, those who indelibly mark your spirit for all times.

"This is why pigs can enter non-Knowing. A place where conscious thought exists no more, but all knowledge is accessible to all. You will know of this place, Baby. I have given it to you.

"Gretel sings to the world. She is the heralder of all things for our herd. She is the record keeper through song.

"Sadie is the grand wiser. Being here the longest, she is a fine, golden-silver thread of all-Knowing for our herd.

"Sweetie is the lost longer, who shows that all pigs belong to each other. Lost from his herd, he longed to belong to ours.

"Abby is the herd protector. She is the keeper of safety.

"Tina is the herd echoer. She spills out memories of your herd when she feels well. She will always be this while she is of hardness.

"The boars are here to keep the species alive and well. They offer strength and companionship, but not much more.

"And Ethel is a record keeper. Need I say more?

"These are the things that you will always be of. No matter where you go, you are here and there. You are herd and we are all one.

"When Ruth asks of you to give your name, be sure to know all of these things in your heart. You will take us with you, one and all.

"And we will all want for you to go, and come again, and always be of us.

Mother"

The Forever:

Not all animals are heard as Tissy was, because most people don't stop to listen. It seems to me that she spoke not for the benefit of the humans around her, rather for her piglets, both before they were born, and then after.

Living on a ranch as a breeding sow is a job that Tissy obviously took seriously. This message to her baby tells of the purpose of life for this herd. It takes into account both the pig's purpose in life, regarding the humans they will become companions for, and more importantly, it is a story passed down from one generation to the next, telling the purpose of each pig to the herd. No matter where they go, they will always know this as their truth, and I believe this with all my heart.

Before her flight was booked, we decided it was time this littlest piglet gave us her name. Flowers kept coming to mind as I tried to "hear" what name she wanted for herself, so I opened an herb book, complete with pictures, and started trying out the names in the hopes she would shout, "That's it!"

Before long, Pennyroyal seemed stuck in my mind, but without being a sure fit. I called Wayne to ask him what he thought.

"Oh no," he said. "How about Penelope? We can call her Penny for short."

"Perfect," I blurted. "I was thinking of Pennyroyal, but Penelope it is." And as I hung up the phone, a second name spilled out of my mouth before I even had a chance to think: "Penny PigMeadows."

Penny has always seemed to know her name, even from the moment she arrived. I've no doubt it is because this was the one she gave to Ruth before she left, as the Texas wildflowers were in full bloom around Sadie's beloved pig park.

Today Penny still responds to some of the names of her original herd when I sit and say them to her while we are talking. An ear turn or a nudge on the knee gives me the belief that she is thinking of them too as their names are called out loud.

Just after Penny's third birthday, Kathleen asked me to be in her wedding. It had been almost three years since I'd been to Texas, and I was excited to be going back. Not only would this be a festive occasion, but I'd also get to see friends I hadn't seen in a long time, people included.

"I'll be gone just a few days, but guess what? I'll be visiting with Mother." The words fell forth excitedly as I sat on the sofa with Penny, who was napping there.

"I will tell everyone all about you when I'm there, and maybe Gretel will have a new song. What would you like me to tell Mother when I see her?" I softly asked my sleeping pig.

A different kind of feeling began to overtake me. It was a feeling of recognition, mixed with a bit of sadness and a faraway touch. Right away, I wondered if Tissy was alright.

"Do you miss Mother, Penny? Is Mother okay?"

I sat there for a minute or two, stroking Penny's soft bristles while trying to discern exactly what I was feeling. I almost got up to call Kathleen, to ask if Tissy was sick, but I had a consult coming in shortly that I needed to prepare for, and besides, this was just a feeling.

Pushing the feeling aside, I smooched Penny on the snooty before heading to my office while thinking to myself that I probably was just picking up on her displeasure about my impending trip. After all, this would be the first time that I would be leaving Penny behind when I traveled. Surely she would not like it either, joining ranks with the good grudge holders, Harry and Clover.

A month passed. The day before I flew to Texas, I called Kathleen to tell her when she could expect me to arrive at her door. She seemed to have wedding preparations well under control.

Before I hung up, I told her how anxious I was to get there, and how I couldn't wait to tell Tissy and the herd what kind of pampered porcine life Penny was enjoying way up in the cold, wintry north.

"Tissy died, Colleen. Didn't I tell you?"

Kathleen's voice trailed off as she went on to describe how Tissy had become ill a while back, but nothing she did helped her to get well. I sat dumbfounded, and with a great sinking in my heart that surprised me, too.

"No," I quietly uttered. "You didn't tell me. I'm sure you forgot because of the busy schedule you've been keeping. I know planning a wedding at your own home is a lot of work."

I tried not to sound disappointed, as I also tried to understand the feelings I was experiencing. I know that death is not a sad end to life. This is what I have learned most from the animals. I heard myself asking her in a voice that seemed far away, "When did she die, Kathleen?"

"About a month ago," she sighed, her voice trailing off into the distance.

Hanging up the phone, I went to find Penny, wanting to tell her the news I'd just received. As I sat on the floor and began to scratch her rump, words never came but Penny immediately began to show me a scene of the afternoon, a month before, when I told her I'd be seeing Mother soon. I didn't understand then, but I did now. Penny had already known about her mother, and if I had only called Kathleen that day, as those feelings had first urged me to do, I would have known then too, that Tissy was ill or already in heaven.

The message to Penny that Tissy had shared three years before began to creep into my mind, past the tears, to warm my saddened heart. I went to search for the written copy. Reading it again filled me with renewed belief that animals do come with a purpose in life, and a purpose for each other.

It didn't explain to me why Tissy had to get sick and die, or why circumstances would keep me from finding out until weeks after it had happened. To this day I have not heard from Tissy either, although I have no doubt she resides in that heavenly place we all transcend to upon our physical death. But I was not the one who really mattered here, just as I was not the important factor the day I overheard Tissy's responses to Kathleen regarding her farrowing preferences, years before.

Perhaps, as in a mystical encounter with an angelic being, Penny PigMeadows had received word of her mother's crossing. How else would she have known, had Tissy not truly evolved unto the winds of her herd's Knowing? ✎

J.R.

"Hello, Mom.
This is your dog in heaven.
You know, that people-place you talk about?"

Rather surprised at the fluency with which J.R. now spoke, I couldn't help but be reminded of the times he only had a few, sometimes snippy, remarks to make when Louise would ask him a question. Passing it off as perhaps a Jack Russell terrier trait, Louise would always chuckle to herself, and I was sure that she'd soften the message when she repeated it to her mom. You see, J.R. was Louise's mother's dog, but Louise liked to do the inquiring.

The first time I ever spoke to J.R., for Louise and her mom, it was quite an event. I quickly learned that every day J.R. and his buddies had the same routine. On her way to work, Louise would first drive to her mom's house, pick up the dogs, and then drive them to her sister's horse farm, where they could play and run all day.

"Oh, I'm the bus driver, Colleen," she said in that first consultation. "After I get my kitties all set for the day, and myself ready to go, I pick up J.R., Leroy, Benjamin and C.C. from Mom's house and then drive them to the farm. Of course, I talk to them the entire time we're driving, and I always see Leroy in the rearview mirror, giving me those eyes, as if he's saying, 'Please, spare us'."

Laughter rolled out of my mouth, and once I regained some composure I quickly apologized for my uncontrolled outburst.

My own imagination provided ample pictures of what I figured this carfull of dogs plus Louise, offered the average passerby. But what really sparked my laughter was the look Leroy showed me as Louise spoke.

Leroy liked to ride in the back seat, all alone. I'd been told it was so he could stretch out and take a nap on the long, six-minute car trip to the farm. With this in mind, I could see him sitting there, quite politely but crowded by the others, with big droopy eyes he'd roll upwards as Louise got on a roll about the days' upcoming events. The expression was undeniably hysterical. I couldn't help laughing.

"No need to apologize, Colleen," Louise said without taking offense. "I know the animals think I'm nuts. But I love them and just can't keep myself from discussing everything on my mind when we're making our morning trips."

Louise was devoted, for sure, and the animals all knew it. Although I was to speak to her many times about the death of one or another, I always looked forward to our communications. Her relationship and repartee with them remained priceless to me, even when the animals spoke about their crossing.

"Hi, Colleen, it's me," Louise said when I answered the phone one day. The sadness in her voice was quite evident. "I was wondering if you would do a favor for me?"

Agreeing without hesitation, I listened as she explained that J.R. had recently crossed over, and how her mom was still pretty sad. Knowing that feeling all too well herself, Louise asked if I could do a communication with J.R. for her mom, and put it in a letter which she could give to her.

"This way she'll have it to look over and over, Colleen. I know how much my letters from my Samantha, McMurphy and Norman meant to me. Theirs are still hanging on the fridge," she said.

By now, Louise was becoming all too familiar with animals heading to heaven. Her losses had been heavy in the short time I'd known her, but her spirit remained upbeat. Although saddened by J.R.'s death herself, Louise possessed a belief in an afterlife for animals that left her confident that he would have an enlightening message to share, even though he had never been much of a talker. She couldn't have been more right. Soon after we spoke, I sat at my keyboard to put my attention on J.R.

>"I'm glad that Louise wanted me to speak, because even though I didn't talk much when I was with you, I've got a lot to say now.
>
>"Listen, it's okay that you decided to let me go after my big problem," J.R. said as I typed. "I'm sorry about the blood. It was a sad thing for you to see, but you know I don't have to be worried about having snippy manners anymore, because all of the dogs I'm with now look just like me. No kidding!
>
>"Nope, they aren't my mother and littermates, and I'm glad because that would be stupid to want to see them here. I say that because they are still doing fun stuff in your world. That's the way it should be, and I only say this because they aren't done learning their lessons. I'll see them when they come. I can be their greeter.
>
>"Now, I suppose Louise wants to smash around in her mind why I'm here now. That's probably a good thing to do because then she can tell my friends that I'm okay and why. First, accidents do happen. I did not expect what happened to me, but that's okay. If I had expected it, I would have spent my time laying around, being all worried over it. Yup, that's the way it works. You decide what you want to do, you get yourself a nice body to do it in, and you live in the moment. This way, when you've learned your lessons, you get to leave.
>
>"It's true that sometimes we stay longer, even though our lessons have been worked on and done, but most times we leave. Why not? But if we were thinking about it every day, we wouldn't want to leave because, that nice body we picked out, its brain doesn't remember where we came from, or usu-

ally where we are now going to. That way we can't cheat on the test of life.

"When we are faced with a lesson to learn, we can't look back and say, 'Okay, I tried it this way and it didn't work. And I tried it that way and that didn't work ...' See what I mean?

"Even though all of those memories are truly there ～ in that part of us that never dies ～ all we have is a feeling of how we should tackle a lesson, and that isn't cheating. Believe it or not, there was a big meeting one time about this learning and memory stuff, and everyone agreed it was a good plan. Really! So don't be sad for me, Mom. I learned my lessons and I came back home.

"Okay, the lessons I learned: Well, the biggest one that I wanted to work on was about not being a snippy dog. One time I was not a very nice dog. I was angry at people for letting me be hungry. Instead of getting my own food to eat, I let them be the boss of me by only getting my food from them. That whole lifetime I was biting people here and chasing them there. It was pathetic. And these people were trying to give me what I wanted. But I always wanted more.

"You might think I was a wolf, but I wasn't. I was just a family dog. So, this time I wanted to work on that snippiness, and to make it a good lesson, I picked out that nice body you loved because those dogs kind of like to be snippy. It's a hunting thing with them, though. See my point?

"I see that I did a fairly good job with not being snippy, even though I was a little bit. And I didn't have to hunt for my food either! You might laugh when I say that I did a 'fairly good job,' thinking that I did not succeed, but really I did. You see, I wanted to bite people more often and chase the animals too. But I did not do it because it didn't feel quite right. So I tried to be a good dog, and I hope you know that I never wanted to bite you or be snippy to you. I just wanted to be a dog who was loved, even though I really was that way. And you did *love me, just the same.*

"And, tell Louise, who is probably reading this already, that I've seen those cats of hers here. They were in the field, looking into the box I was in, when I first got here. Queeny Samantha is not so snippy herself now, but she still likes to think she's the boss. That's okay. She's earned it. She looks nice all pink, too.

"So, I hope you are alright with me being here. Tell everyone that I'm just fine and that I'm sorry about the blood problem. I couldn't help that, but it didn't really hurt. I cried because I didn't know what was happening. It was a good choice to help me like you did. I would not have been happy at all not being able to walk.

"I want to go now. I'm not much of a talker, you know. Besides, there are nice holes here to go into. I guess I'm still relating to being your J.R. Isn't that funny? You know, I don't have to.

"Oh, and please tell the horses they were great ⁓ And Louise for taking me to see them ⁓ And you for giving me treats all the time. I had a very good life with you, Mom, and even though I wasn't old, it was a life full of experiences that still make me smile.

I'll know you always."
J.R.

Stunned at the volumes J.R. had to say, I laughed as I watched the little terrier zip down a hole and out of sight. Looking over the note, I was intrigued at the reference of blood J.R. had mentioned, because when Louise called, she didn't tell me what had happened to him, only that he was gone.

Stuffing a few sheets of my best stationery into the printer, I checked my final draft, then printed out J.R.'s message to mail to Louise. Two days later she called to say she'd gotten it and how much it had meant to her mother.

"Oh my gosh, Colleen. That J.R., what a talker! No wonder he never said much while he was here. He must have been saving it all up."

"What was that mention about blood?" I asked her, still wondering. "What happened to him?"

"Well, Colleen, it was really strange," Louise began. "We're not sure what happened because one day he appeared to be just fine, then the next day he didn't move at all. Later that same day we found blood all over the stairs and he was getting cold.

"We took him to the vet immediately, and he looked like he was still with us. But before the vet could do much, J.R. passed away on his own. We never found out what had really happened."

Louise and I talked about many things that day, and although she had already done so, we talked with each of J.R.'s friends again, repeating his message of how he was just fine now.

"It's funny how much the animals enrich our lives while here, with their unconditional love," Louise said to me in closing, "and how they can comfort us in our grief, even when it's them that we are grieving for."

I agreed.

"That J.R.," she mused. "I sure will miss him on our morning drive to the farm."

With that said, we both bid our farewells, each hoping that our next communication would be more joyous. ❧

Montana's Rose

"A horse is more than just a friend
who carries you through life,
A horse is someone you can trust,
to love you always ⁓ 'til the end ..."

The power of unconditional love never ceases to amaze me, and in the early spring of 1999, I was amazed yet again during a series of touching moments between two humans and their incredible horses.

I met Denise and Dean Rose at the Police Olympics, where I served as a volunteer at the equestrian events. My sister, Maureen, a mounted police officer, introduced us that day, and we've been friends ever since. It was always exciting for me to be at these events because not only did I get to meet Mo's partners, like Dean, but also the Mounties' real partners: the horses themselves. Conversing with intelligent beings is always a joy for me, but being surrounded by these incredible service animals always added an element of thrill. Police horses are their very own special breed.

Several years later, when budget cutbacks forced an end to the Mounted Patrol, I spoke with each horse, and the police pony as they prepared to disband. The horses stood quietly on cross-ties for one last official grooming. Everyone there found it hard to say good-bye as they each left for their last detail ⁓ the one that would take them to new stables and new lives. All had earned a well-deserved retirement.

I wondered if any of the horses, or their mounts, would ever really know how large a loss the city was facing, now that these familiar and welcome faces would no longer be seen on our streets. It was a sad day for Syracuse, but also day of celebration for their service well done.

Captain Duster went home with his partner, Dean, and immediately became the love of Denise's life. At 22 years old, Dusty was ready for a leisurely palomino retirement, but Dean had found that having Dusty at home got him anxious to get back into serious riding again, maybe even some showing. Because a horse needs a herd, their family soon grew yet again when Dean's sister contributed the "family horse." Montana's Rose arrived soon after.

From the moment that thoroughbred hoof first hit the ground, as he emerged from the trailer on that hot June day, Montana began enriching their lives in ways most would never dream of. You see, Dusty and Montana, although destined to be great friends, were as opposite as night and day.

Dusty, accustomed to police work and changing situations, could stand for hours on or off cross-ties, while his new, novice horse-mom fussed on him or dressed him up. It would be more than three years before Denise would ever get on Dusty to ride him, but she was there every day for hours, tending to her horse.

Montana, on the other hand, had spent most of his 12 years at a huge riding facility, where many riders came and went. If he wasn't eating his grain or working with a rider, he was turned out to pasture with the other horses, which suited him just fine. Denise and Dean quickly learned that Montana could not be cross-tied, nor could a fly mask be put on him. Accident-prone and high-spirited, he soon learned how to take advantage of a novice. But Denise persevered, every day tending to Montana's wants and needs as best she could.

Though he dragged her in from the pasture a few times, pushed her around as she learned the ropes, sprained her pinky finger so badly it remained permanently crooked, and ignored her completely when Dean was there, setbacks were few and made no real difference to my dedicated friend. She still gave Montana the same unconditional love she gave Dusty daily, because after all, these horses were now part of their family ∼ their children.

In the four years since Montana & Dusty became "herd," I have spoken countless times with Denise and the horses. The conversations we've had with "the boys" usually revolved around new tack or supplies they might like or need, or what they would like put on the new name-plates being made to grace their stall doors. Each horse always gave thoughtful advice, and Denise always did her best to accommodate their wishes ... right down to the holiday decorations they'd like to see hanging about their area. But I must say my favorite topic was always what costumes they'd like to wear each Halloween.

My favorite picture of Montana is the one of him standing serenely on cross-ties late one October, dressed up as his vet. Highlighting his growing reputation as the "Boo-boo King," Montana is complete with face mask, hat, scrubs and hoof covers. He also wore a name tag, next to the stethoscope dangling from his neck. So although we were not surprised when he won first prize at the animal hospital's pet photo contest later that same year, many mouths still dropped to the floor when they got a load of the horse ready for trick-or-treating.

Shortly after Montana's 16th birthday, my daughter Sarah heard a call come in on the office answering machine, then came quickly to find me. "Mom, Denise just called. She said Montana broke his leg."

My heart instantly sank as I gathered my wits about me and headed for the phone. Before I finished dialing, I was tuned in to Montana, and I knew that what he had begun sharing with me was not good.

"I put them in the indoor arena like always, then I went off to do some chores," Denise explained. "After a little while, I had the feeling that I should go back. When I rounded the corner, Montana nickered a look-what-I-did nicker to me, and he stood there holding his leg up. I knew right away that it was broken."

Dean had already arrived, as had one of the vets. They were with Montana right then, talking about what could be done. The severe break appeared to be irreparable. They'd been discussing taking him to Cornell for surgery, as well as euthanasia. As they waited for the other vet to arrive, Denise wanted to ask Montana what he wanted. I tuned in to her injured friend.

"I was not kicked," he assured me, and it seemed important to him that this be known. Pictures of him bucking playfully started forming in my mind, then suddenly he fell. All the while Dusty stood by patiently, watching him.

"I am not afraid to go," Montana also said, as both Denise and I choked back our tears. Then Denise saw the other vet had arrived, and it seemed to her that some decision had been made based on everyone's movements. As Denise hung up the phone and hurried back to Montana, I walked to the other room to sit next to my husband on the sofa.

"Could you send Montana some loving thoughts and energy with me, right now, please?" I asked Wayne.

Although overcome with sadness for my friends and myself, the tears streaming down my face did not obscure the pictures Montana continued to send. With eyes closed and my husband's comforting hand upon my shoulder, I took in every detail of what Montana wished to share.

He was calmer now, disassociated from the great pain his body would be feeling. Any fear one might expect was absent. Clearly, I watched him nuzzle his face into Denise's long hair, as if to smell it one more time. As I breathed in deeply, a cherished scent, which must be all her own, filled my nostrils, while a loving, comforting feeling filled the rest of me. As if a spell had been cast, we both paused to savor this blissful moment.

Then, as if to both give and receive some kind of inner fortitude, Montana dropped his head into Dean's stomach, holding it there steadily. A warmth of anesthesia began to rise up my back from below, and I could feel the once incredible strength of Montana begin to ebb like the tide. It moved slowly and evenly around my ribs, then into my stomach. A slight feeling of nausea briefly passed by, and Montana buried his face even deeper into Dean's jacket. The warmth continued to ascend up my back, slowly passing over the top of my head.

As if I were drifting off into dreamland, my view dimmed briefly as the anesthetic warmth reached my forehead, but only for a fleeting moment. Startled by a sudden flash, I watched Montana move his head as if in slow motion. He began to turn away from Dean.

The serenity of the vision I'd been immersed in instantly transformed into the thrill of anticipation, as though I were at a starting-gate opening. Like an explosion, Montana was off in a full-blown gallop, and the exultation was like a breath of life that I have never known.

"The wind in my mane is a wonderful thing!"

I cried out from the incredible rush of freedom that suddenly flooded over me, and I realized what it meant ∽ my friend Montana had just crossed over to the Rainbow Bridge.

These were to be the last words I would ever "hear" Montana say. But for three whole days after his crossing, I watched him gallop through fields of wildflowers and along the water's edge, never slowing once and never looking back. His mane flew freely in the wind, and his tail waved a blissful farewell.

When his crossing was confirmed a short time later, I shared with Denise all of the details I'd seen from my living room, more than forty miles from his stable. As I spoke of my experience, I realized Montana was giving a gift he meant to share not only with his family, but also with me. It's a gift I will always cherish.

It seemed to me that the many minute details Montana shared that night were meant not only to comfort his family and himself, but also to serve as his own special "thank you" to me for all I had offered him over the years. The homeopathic care that helped ease his various aches and pains during his reign as the Boo-boo King was just a fragment of our relationship. I believe Montana most appreciated the voice I'd lent him, the one with which he could truly be heard.

Picturing Montana galloping toward the Rainbow Bridge served as a blessing to Denise and Dean, who truly believe in a heaven for horses. This place, I've learned, horses call the "Forever Green," where the pastures are filled with wildflowers, and where horses live forever.

Montana's last worldly utterance evoked smiles to break through their tears as they remembered a time, not long ago, when Montana had jumped the paddock fence into the forbidden pasture where the wildflowers grew.

Today, Montana's beloved wildflowers grow on his grave, which overlooks the beautiful lake he saw every day from his pasture not far away

~ a peaceful setting for a spirited horse. His herdmate, Dusty, managed through Montana's death better than we had expected, perhaps because he'd had the opportunity to be with his friend that night, and was allowed to say his own good-bye to Montana before he was led away.

In the few weeks after Montana's physical death, Dusty carefully prepared his own special eulogy for his good friend who'd gone on before him. When he was ready, he let me know, then his message was printed onto special cards, a special "thank you" to those who'd filled Montana's empty stall with flowers, bringing comfort in a time of need. Perhaps it will have meaning to all who share their life with horses. One thing I know for sure, this palomino called Dusty, and his friend, Montana's Rose, will live on in many hearts, for many years to come.

"A horse is more than just a friend
who carries you through life,
A horse is someone you can trust,
to love you always ~ 'til the end.
A horse is more than just a friend
you visit now and then,
Your horse is an extension
of the love you've given him.

A horse's friend will be there,
always looking deep within,
and will seek to make him happier,
by understanding who he is.
Life's lessons spent together,
and in learning how to be a pair,
will be moments unforgotten ...
Memories you both will share.

And when life leads us to the fields
we call Forever Green,
we take with us the love you gave,
and carry it beyond our grave.

A horse's friend is someone
who'll then give themselves a chance,
to open up their heart, once more,
and learn to love again.

"Each tear that's shed for horses
who had lived and loved a man,
are tears that honour who we were,
and what we gave back in return.

"Storms are just a passing wind,
tho' how the winds can blow,
But a horse's friend will weather through,
like the winds that moved Montana's Rose.

Captain Duster, Mounted Patrol, Retired.
City of Syracuse Police Department"

⮑

Tom

"Hello Tom," I began, as I established a link with this cat who had recently crossed over. "My name is Colleen, and your mom asked me to speak to you. She would like to know if you are well in your new life. And, she would also like to know if you have any message for her. So Tom, will you speak? Will you tell me your truth?"

"Dear Mother,
Although it has been a while since I arrived here, do not think that I am not still having a wonderful time..."

Tom Cat began the message to his mom with a tenderness all his own. Once a big, white feline, he charmed me instantly as he began to pour thoughts, feelings and words into my head, even before I had a chance to get my fingers to the keyboard. Never having spoken with Tom before, I did not expect things to begin so quickly. However, captivated from the start, I could barely wait for his next thought to appear, which did not take long.

In the midst of my busy days communicating with animals both near and far, sometimes a call comes in requesting that I speak with one who has already passed away, and with whom I've never spoken before. Although this does not make the communication any harder to do, it does leave me feeling a bit more like a psychic than an animal communicator, which I feel are two different things.

Communicating with an animal who is alive, on my plane of existence, is done via telepathy, something everyone is capable of doing but, it seems, most of us have merely forgotten how.

Communicating with an animal who no longer inhabits a physical body is usually telepathic for me too, although sometimes I'm considered a psychic when working in this capacity. Not knowing if or where a line can be drawn distinguishing the two, I do know that in Tom's case it was pure animal communicating at its finest.

Nothing spooky or hair-raising occurred that day, as I'll sometimes find associated with the psychic realm. It was just a typical communication link with Tom, but the speed with which it came, and the message within, left me astonished at what this cat had to say.

Tom spoke with clarity and purpose, his message coming almost faster than I was capable of taking down. His words flowed like a mountain stream headed to the valley below. Once started, there simply was no stopping it.

"Do you remember when I was a young cat and could be busy all day long? I am feeling this way again, and no, it is not the cliche of 'eternal youth in heaven.' Rather it is just the wonderfulness of being 'me' forever.

"During the time we spent together, you gave me much respect. Even though you did not always understand me, nor I you, we were a good pair of friends, don't you think? I always loved the way you gave me space, and you loved to look at me ⁓ the most handsome Tom Cat ever. I am sure I was better to have around than just another dog.

"When I am asked, 'Tom, will you tell me your truth?' I answer that I will be happy to do just that. My truth is that I am thankful you let me come back home, here, in an easy way, even though it was hard for you.

"My truth is too that it was okay for me to get old like that, because it was for a very short time. Most of our lives are spent where I am now. Here, I am my true self. With you, I was but an expression of life.

"My truth is that I will look for you again. I don't know when, but Beings like to stay together, through what seems to be good or bad, easy or hard, happy or sad. It's just a big story, and I will soon decide what my next story will be. I may decide to try something very different. I may not be a cat.

"My truth is, too, that I will always be your Tom. Even though I am just a memory in your story now, I am a memory that lives in your heart. Because of this, my story has greater meaning. My story will be told for longer times yet to come, for as you speak my name ∼ if only in your thoughts ∼ I am reborn in legend, and you know that legends live a very long time on Earth. And did you know that legends can help you decide what your next story might be? It's true.

"So, even though I will look for you again, it will seem like a long time to you, although it won't seem long to me. I will wait until my legend is clear enough that it helps me decide my next story.

"And my truth is too that my story will be my life. A story born in heaven, manifested on Earth, allowing it to flourish in whatever way seems most plausible, then transcends into heaven to become yet another story of who we all are.

"Given this long cat tale, isn't it hard to believe that I'm just here chasing red felt mice?

"Thank you for my story with you.
Your loving cat,
Tom"

When communications come this way, I am always excited and extremely grateful. I'm left with no doubt in my mind that the message being received is indeed coming from one poised in a place with a far greater vantage point from which to see than mine is here on Earth. There's a comfort in this, for me.

When Tom finished, I was left to wonder what Cecilia, Tom's grieving human mom, would think. I also wondered about the special relationship and deep bond they must have shared.

Confident that I could never have "imagined" such wisdom as the cat had conveyed, I slid Tom's message into a special card and mailed it to Cecilia. I never did hear back from her, but I did from someone else ∽ Louise called to say that her sister, C.C., had shared Tom's message with her. They both had a good cry and through it I hope Cecelia found learning to live without Tom a little easier to do. ✋

Sometimes they just think

about it...

Chapter 4

Clue

*"My face is gray 'cause I'm old.
I'm feeling like a very old horse …
I am now."*

Clue had arrived at the hospital in grave condition, and was immediately put into the equine center's Intensive Care Unit. The 20-year-old companion animal of Gillian, a young, interning veterinarian, now had some of the best veterinary minds in the country to look after him. Quickly, they began the tests they hoped would reveal just what was wrong with Clue and how they could best help him get well.

I met some wonderful people at Cornell's Large Animal and Equine Veterinary Center when my friend, Chrissy Pig, spent 12 days there a while back. They were full of a special love for the animals, gave selflessly to those in their charge, and obviously shared a deep commitment to animals in general. Like Gillian, they all had companion animals at home, too.

In a quiet moment in Chrissy's stall one day, I had laughed with Gillian as she told me how, while working for a local veterinarian, she passed out at least once a week for years before going to college to become the veterinarian she is today.

"They would just pick me up and laugh, and I'd be so embarrassed," she said, giggling shyly and patting Chrissy on the hams as she rose. "I haven't fainted in a long time now, though."

When I learned of Clue's arrival at Cornell and Gillian's devastation at her companion's prognosis, I sat down to contemplate whether there was anything that I could do to help. Instantly I could see the gray of Clue's face and began to write down his message. It was not what I expected. I'd hoped Clue could tell me exactly where he hurt and just what was wrong, but he had something even more important to say.

> *"She is so sad. Red eyes and short respirations. I can't tell her, Breathe deep. I am here and I can see you."*

Right away I was sure, beyond a doubt, that it was Clue who was speaking to me. His description of Gillian's sorrow was spoken like only a true veterinarian's horse.

> *"She needs to know I see her. I will always see her. Even when she is far away. Even when I am too."*

My heart sank at the thought that Clue was contemplating crossing over. As though he could feel my sorrow for Gillian's coming loss, he carefully moved on, formulating words to express what his life with her has meant to him.

> *"When I am in my stall, I think about the things that make me smile inside. Gilly's hair and her giggle, her shoes, and that dog. This is what I do when I stand and think. I think too, about the time we ride, although now all we do is walk.*
>
> *"I want there to be beauty in Gilly's mind when I gallop to the pasture ∼ the one that will be forever green, and not like the one here that withers when it's cold. And I want there to be lasting memories in Gilly's heart, because this is where all good resides. She is young and healthy and full of life. The good will live there a long, long time.*
>
> *"Many horses and cows and pigs and dogs and cats and others will come her way. There will be much to do to*

help them move on, and moving on will not always be as she'd like it to be. But perhaps it's because she hasn't seen me move on, therefore she doesn't know how beautiful life really is.

"In Gilly's mind, death can be a welcome relief, and this is true for the sick and maimed. But it is my belief, from the 'Knowing' of herd, which all horses have from the time they are born, that death can also be that release to the greatest of beauty these eyes here can't even begin to see. A rose is not really a rose when viewed from the Biggest of Unfenced Pastures. A rose is but a colour of light, a beacon, to whoever has heavenly eyes with which to see.

"Here in my stall, a rose would be a small, beautiful flower, no bigger than your hand. Where horses go upon leaving this realm, roses grow whose colour lights up the sky, each one more beautiful than the next. Gilly's eyes are the colour of roses now. In heaven, the place where horses one day go, her eyes are the colour of love. When she cries, it is the sound of a love song, but here and now it feels like the sound of the greatest sadness.

"Let there be no great sadness in your cry, Gilly. Let your cry be of the joy we've shared here together.

"My life as your horse has given me purpose. Purpose of ride and pleasure and connectedness to a joyful time. Your life with me has given you happiness and nurture, release from a weary mind and body, a time to relax into the rhythm of nature and its oneness. Humans are quick to forget that all-important rhythm, but it is the rhythm of life and should not be ignored. Those who live in its presence are forever endowed with the determination to look forward and the drive to endure.

"Humans who love horses carry the spirit of the wind. It always blows across the lands and will always carry them forward. Gilly will always hear me in the wind ∽ she will always smell me in the breeze ∽ and this same wind or gentle breeze will dry her tears, then rustle the rose, as it looks for *new places across the land in which to bloom again.*

"My mother taught me to look to the pasture and to know inside that it will be there, always, as will I … as will all horses born into this realm. This pasture you call heaven, we call the 'Forever Green,' and we are carried to and from it on winds of love.

"Know in your heart, Gilly, that I have come before and I will come again. This is the way we horses are ∽ there really is no end. And when you stand by a being in need and are not sure what to do, say to yourself, 'I haven't a Clue.' And then giggle, because you do. I will always be in the breeze.

"Thank you for asking me to speak.
Clue"

Clue left Cornell about a week after he arrived. Gillian wrote to say that the tests done had been inconclusive, and she was just going to spend time with her beloved friend, taking it one day at a time. As I write this, one month after his hospital release, he continues to improve slowly. One day, time may tell what was wrong, and whether he'll fully recover. One thing is for sure, Gillian will not look at death the same way again. No matter where life finds her down the road, she'll always have a Clue as to where she's headed. ✧

An Old Aborigine Philosophy

"Our purpose here is to observe, to learn, to grow, to love, and then we return Home."

There are many different conditions that cause life here to transcend into the next stage of living. It could be illness, an accident, old age, cruelty, slaughter, or simply a choice. Whichever way "death" occurs, my experiences have shown me that at the moment of passing, the emotions we cling to as humans vanish … at least in the animal kingdom they do.

In the 1970s, a book titled *Life After Life*, by Dr. Raymond Moody, brought to light a human phenomenon that dates back to ancient times, the Near Death Experience, NDE. He had researched and logged hundreds of accounts of experiences people had had while clinically dead, before being revived.

Moody found continuity in his subjects' incredible experiences and remarkable similarities. Often they involved a tunnel, a magnificent being of light who poured overwhelming love or knowledge into them, the ability to view their body from above or beside it, the experience of being greeted by others who had died before them, and a sadness at having to return to their physical body. People who'd had an NDE were changed forever by the experience of death. They were no longer afraid to die, as they had experienced life on the other side and knew that it was nothing to be afraid of because nothing really ended, it only transformed into something more beautiful.

Work done by other researchers into the near death experience has shown that during the dying process negative emotions such as fear, anger and loneliness are replaced by the positive emotions of peace, love and utter joy. Again, the only sadness that people experienced usually occurred upon realizing that they had to come back to their body for some reason.

A *Turning Point* broadcast in September of 1997 titled, "Death: A Doorway to Joy" shed light on just how widespread this phenomenon of near death experience truly is. It stated that there are seven million people in the United States who have experienced an NDE. A shockingly high figure, isn't it? It is attributed to the medical technologies of our times, giving us the ability to revive people who would have surely died otherwise. With modern life-saving technologies also comes the technological ability to physically chart electrical and chemical activity associated with a near death trauma.

Some scientists discredit the reality of NDE, referring to it as a hallucination of a dying brain. They rationalize it as the body's way of calming itself down by inducing calming visions, helping to protect itself during trauma or extreme stress. That same extreme stress will produce endorphins, which in their opinion are responsible for the visions, as they are typically associated with a warm, high, euphoric feeling that you may have heard referred to as "runner's high."

However, the most extensive research that has been done on NDEs, supporting their validity and reality came from 12 Dutch hospitals. They found many of their patients were able to recount information they couldn't possibly have known, things such as occurrences or words said in the hallway or in another room. They couldn't possibly have been heard or seen. These experiences support the claims of those seven million Americans who have shared a common vision of the truth that this is not the only life we will have or live.

My work with animals has shown me that they experience these same feelings of joy and happiness at returning to the nonphysical state. One difference that I have found is that animals are often prepared for their crossing, and many of these emotions are experienced as they prepare to go. Although I do not recall them referring to a tunnel of light, they often share visions with me of misty brightness, into which beings begin to take form ∼ beings that are benevolent ∼ oftentimes beings from their life here.

Once on the other side of life, suffering seems to cease instantly for them as well. Joy and happiness are oftentimes overwhelming, and love exudes from every ion of their being. They achieve a new viewpoint and with it, peace.

As a communicator who is the link between a family member and the animal they have lost, I often receive messages referring to information that I could not possibly have known. Whether communicating a favorite memory that they have taken with them, helping their humans locate their favorite place for a resting memorial or decide what the memorial should be, I find being able to receive such information is quite rewarding both for me and for the loved ones left behind.

The most beautiful gifts in life are said to be the ones we can take with us when we leave. The "continuity" that I have found when working in this realm is that the animals carry with them all of love we gave. The times we have spent playing ball, sitting quietly together, gazing into each other's eyes, or even singing to them, become cherished memories that stay with them always ∼ undying acts of kindness and respect.

Chrissy Pig

"Chrissy is my hero," Mo said.
And, through the years, I've heard it more than once.

Chrissy Pig is my sister Maureen's companion, and she gave us a good example of this when she once shared a favorite memory, one that may transcend time and space. A beautiful white potbelly pig, Chrissy picked Mo as a companion on our first trip to Texas a year before. I had gone to teach animal communication at a seminar sponsored by the North American Potbelly Pig Association. Afterwards we traveled to Kathleen's, a new friend whose pig park would become a very special place for me over the coming years.

It was quite a sight. About 40 pigs greeted us as we walked through the gates, many of them tipping over in hopes of a belly rub or two. I wandered through the pig park reaching down to pat as many pigs as I could, completely in awe at the marvelous little animals before me. These pigs were not aloof like my own two boys at home, and it was thrilling to be able to touch and pat each one without them running away. I did not get to pat Chrissy Pig, though, as she had found Mo in the crowd and followed her every move.

"I would be walking through the herd, and I could sense someone following me," Mo says whenever anyone asks how Chrissy came to be her pig. To me there was no doubt her police officer training was working overtime while on vacation.

"When I would stop and turn around, that all-white Chrissy Pig would stop in her tracks and just stare at me. She did this for the two whole days we were there!"

Before we left it was brought to light that this was not typical behavior for Chrissy, nor did she follow anyone else that weekend. It was just Maureen, and Chrissy really wanted to be with her.

We returned to Texas the following winter, I to work and Maureen to vacation. As we approached the pig park, pigs gathered near the gate. But the best sight was that of Chrissy Pig running across the yard, her lavender bow flopping up and down on her head and her potbelly swinging from side to side as she hurried to Maureen. A week later, on Valentine's Day, it was decided that Chrissy Pig would come to New York.

Two months later, and the day before my 40th "Earth Day" birthday, Chrissy Pig, Iris and Penny PigMeadows arrived at the airport in Syracuse. Many were there to greet them. I traveled in the back of a truck with Chrissy the short distance to her new farm, where she and Iris would enjoy a creekside abode in nice weather and an indoor condo during the cold winter months, which would be a big change for these southern belles. Penny PigMeadows came home with me. I was in great need of a snuggly pig, so she was my birthday present from both my husband and my good friend Kathleen, who had raised this Texas herd.

While visiting the farm on Mother's Day, about a month after they arrived, we noticed that Chrissy was not acting well. At first we thought she was having trouble adjusting to her new home away from the only herd she had ever known. The piglets, Penny and her sister Iris, had done just fine, but Chrissy was four, and we wondered if that had made the transition harder.

As it turned out, Chrissy was very ill and had been sick for a long time. By the time the veterinarians at Cornell found the cause, she was near death and required emergency surgery. She survived the surgery, but with many concerns and worries by her surgeon.

Chrissy Pig had a severe pyometra that had traveled up her fallopian tube and completely destroyed her right ovary. As they tried to remove it, carefully peeling away the diseased layers, a tear was found in her bowel. A resection was done, but the surgeon worried about the apparent lack of blood supply to the anestamosis site. Although it didn't look right to her, they had to close because Chrissy was starting to fail on the table. After she awoke from anesthesia, Chrissy walked back to her stall, and a sleepless night was had by all.

The next morning we arrived to find Chrissy lying outside in the early spring sunshine with veterinary medical students and doctors gathered around her. I got out the lawn chairs and a blanket while Maureen sat on the ground, loving on her pig and softly singing her favorite song. Chrissy Pig sighed ∼ a big sigh ∼ then said as clear as day, "You know, if things don't work out, I will take *this* with me."

Chrissy underwent one more surgery, but not before she had her own input as to what was to be allowed and when to let her go, if need be. Potbelly pigs do not do well with anesthesia and this would be her third in five days. We worried that she would not survive the anesthesia, much less another surgery. We wiped our tears away as we each kissed her snooty before she was wheeled down the hall to the operating room. After she disappeared from sight, Maureen reminded me what was in her own heart:

"I just can't believe that Chrissy worked so hard to come to New York just to die." And she didn't.

Today she is a healthy, happy companion pig who always reminds us that unconditional love is the strongest love of all, and that what is in our hearts is what truly matters when we leave. ✎

Gilby, Comanche and the Wild Horses

"To kill a Mustang ⌒ stable it," Gilby said,
quite matter-of-factly.

Feeling both privileged and excited to speak with a herd of Mustangs, I was amazed at the difference between these once wild horses and their domesticated kin. A sensation of bursting wide open filled my chest, triggered by a new feeling: the run of the wild. It left me in awe of these magnificent beings. Most amazing to me, these Mustangs had not been in the wild for a number of years.

It was always like Josie (who had used other communicators before me) to inquire about nearly every horse in the barn, whenever she called me to speak with her own two horses, Ricochet and Prince. Perhaps this is why her friend's Mustangs, Gilby and Roberta, spoke so easily with me. Either way, horses have always been a favorite of mine to work with, along with pigs. Their great intelligence and offerings of wisdom are always incredibly enlightening and thought provoking. I've yet to meet a horse or a pig who didn't have something amazing to say, and these Mustangs were no exception.

When Josie simply asked how they were doing, many of the "feelings" they conveyed seemed multifaceted, more intense. For example,

Gilby and Roberta showed me their favorite colours: those of sunsets over vast, open spaces. The Mustangs still held dear their own memories of such sights, even though Ohio sunsets were probably not quite the same. Roberta's yearling, Zosha, said her favorite colour was that of the autumn wind, while showing me coloured leaves falling to the ground as breezes blew them from the trees. Her playfulness welled within me, along with a deep respect for a "wild" she was only born with and not to.

The most intense feelings I received during our talk were those regarding wildness. "Herd" had a much deeper feeling of connectedness for all of these wild horses. Herd is important to other horses as well, but generally not to the degree of depth that it seemed to go in these Mustangs. I wondered if that was because other horses usually spent their lives being bought and sold for their various attributes.

Wanting to share the Mustangs' feelings, the next day I e-mailed a new friend in California, whose own two Mustangs had never spoken with me before. As always, I was surprised and amazed at what transpired.

"It's different from regular horses," I wrote her. "For these three, *herd* means much, much more."

"This is exactly why I worry so much about Comanche and Heritage," PJ replied. "When the time comes and one of them dies, what will the other do? They have never been apart?"

"They're so connected to each other. On the plains, they lived with hundreds of other Mustangs. We picked two yearlings out of the herd, and they became lifelong companions. Since then, they've known no other horses but themselves."

As I read her message, the words on the page started to disappear as Comanche began to speak to me. Surprised, I grabbed a pen and pad and began to write down their message.

> *"I want to tell you that the life we have is special to us. Heritage and I are herd and you are herd, too. We thank you for remembering our wildness.*
>
> *"There was a time when I was hungry and sick, yet I did not fear. We do not live in those moments, for they have*

passed. We live for today and tomorrow.

"One day, when Heritage or I rejoin our mothers in spirit, it will be of great joy, it is true, for the traveler. The last whinny we'll hear will be our herdmate's farewell. Our first sight after that will be the lighted wild ones who have gone on before us. And we won't look back, as horses never do. The one left behind will not either. The one left behind will look to today and tomorrow and will live in the moment of our people herd.

"You have given us a gift that will always live on ⌣ dignity, for the wild we once were and still hold in our hearts. Though we've not had mountains to gallop or streams to drink from, we still live on a hill and the sky never ends. We have shelter and water and love from our people. We have joyous times and reflective times when we enjoy who we are. We did not know this as babies who left our mothers' sides, but we learned this as horses, your companions of a large kind.

"Remember this thought as we whisper our truth: the respect you have showed us since our wild youth, we have happily looked out upon as a gift in our life.

"When we leave, we will know that we take with us too, more than the wild horses … with us, we'll take you.

Comanche"

At 22 years old, suffering only from an occasional touch of arthritis, Comanche and Heritage live in the hills of California with PJ and her family. With, I believe, many years left yet to enjoy, facing the inevitable will be a little bit easier for PJ and her family, now that these Mustangs have spoken.

I have come to realize that when animals are treated with respect for who they are, the deepest of bonds is created between man and beast. "To kill a Mustang …," as Gilby said is, I believe, to kill the beautiful, wild spirit that the Mustang is endowed with at birth.

Gilby and his herd still enjoy wide open spaces, as much as their Ohio farm allows. Even though they are sometimes stabled at night, their humans' regard for their "wild" is what sustains them the most. Respect for one another ∼ even across species ∼ is both cherished and sustaining. Something you can take with you, when you go.↩

Millie

"This is not home for us ...
It is just a rest stop upon a long journey."

These soothing words, from one old friend to another, came softly one day. To me, the most touching thing about them is that these words came from a goat named Millie, and she was trying to help her human deal with a loss which was now upon the horizon.

Aging without grace is a difficult thing for most humans to watch any loved one endure, and my friend Becky was no exception. Millie was an older goat who seemed wiser than her mere mortal years, and her health had been declining for some time. But in spite of her physical ailments, Millie looked at life differently than Becky did, and in the hopes that the inevitable departure would be easier for Becky to bear, Millie offered many comforting words. She also wanted to offer some helpful suggestions regarding the subsequent care of Vicky, her herdmate.

"Yes, I am feeling somewhat better, thank you for asking..." she began. Then slowly Millie began to outline how she thought Vicky could best be attended to in her first days of life alone. She spoke of Ignatia, a homeopathic remedy that should be given to Vicky to help heal the grief, and discussed living options that could be looked into, because a goat needs a herd. Then, after having satisfied her maternal instincts, she turned her attention to Becky, who wanted to do anything she could to extend Millie's life, if only for just a little bit longer. Millie spoke quietly.

> *"There are many times in this world where a lifetime seemingly ends, in your eyes, and you do not see it is rejoiced in the lighted worlds. It's almost like stopping somewhere to gather enough sustenance, before moving on to the next destination. I know that you understand what I mean because you have done this yourself.*
>
> *"In the rescue work that you do for us all, there are times when you are truly helping, yet other times you are interfering with a preordained departure, so here you should remember that not all of us have come to be saved. Preparing in your heart for this, so that you may let go when the time is right, is just as important as the rescuing that you do. You know, Becky, a soft heart has every right to be a strong one. Look inside your chest, at your real heart, and feel the lightness of letting go when the time is right. If you listen with your lighted heart, you will know the difference. **There are no good-byes … There are only Welcome Homes.***
>
> *Millie"*

It was very interesting to me that Millie seemed to believe in fate, preordained experiences that animals would be subjected to. Perhaps in Millie's eyes, Becky was trying to avoid the inevitable, and Millie plainly felt she needn't do so. Whatever life had to offer, Millie was not afraid to encounter it, whether in this world or the next.

Millie enjoyed her "Welcome Home" shortly after this communication. Vicky got her remedy for grief, along with a new little goat whom she promptly named Bobby. Becky cried, and life went on.

Becky currently shares her life with over 40 animals. Recently the losses have been many, but that is how it goes when you've rescued "throwaway" animals, those who started life under dreadful conditions. Many times the love and support you give them, both physically and emotionally, are not enough to mend both broken bodies and spirits, giving way to shortened lifespans. Inner peace needs to come from knowing that you've done all you could.

"In some ways, the losses are made easier to deal with when you know that those who have crossed over are now happy, whole and no longer in pain," Becky told me when I inquired one day as to how animal communication had helped her to deal with the physical loss.

"Sometimes it's harder for me, because I've gotten to know them on a much deeper level. It's almost like losing your grandmother," Becky said. "I'd rather not have to lose them at all, but that's not realistic.

"Knowing them each as a real individual, like I knew Millie, is better for us both while they are here, but I still miss them awfully when they're gone."

I sighed with understanding, thinking back to the losses my own life has endured. But Millie's words echoed back in my mind, *There are no good-byes … There are only Welcome Homes."*

Sometimes there's
no real reason…

The Golden Rule

"Do unto others
as you would have them do unto you."

I believe that the arrogance of our own species is our downfall, at best. Supposedly smartest of all animals upon this planet, just three rungs on the intelligence ladder above pigs, for a civilized species we have not done very well. On the whole as a society we have put our own needs, wants and desires above everything else, and our planet shows the sad marks of our actions. As the cause of raging wars to the wasting of natural resources and the blatant destruction of areas of Earth, like the rainforest that is critical to our very survival, humans appear to have a very selfish purpose in life. How did we come to this?

At least when two humans are involved in an issue, both have a voice. Even though one may be small and weak, at least it can be heard. However, when a human and an animal are the parties involved, it often seems too easy to blow off doing the right thing because of the old myth that animals can't talk. In fact, many people still believe that animals have no feelings, or even a soul. This pitiful belief structure seems to give some people justification to either accept, allow, excuse or encourage animal abuse.

Nothing is sadder to me than when a conscious decision is made to disregard another's well-being. It seems to me that most often the reason given is because it is either not convenient, would cost a little money, or is a bit more effort than one cares to put out. In my work, too often I see the end result. It's a very sad story indeed, and the animal always pays the bigger price.

I expect some will say that the real crimes in the world don't involve animals, but are the ones we commit against each other. Too often, women are sexual prey. Men abuse others, often having been abused themselves. Too many are the victims of violence, and children are killing children. We all feel small and helpless when looking into the face of Society and her enormous problems, but can just one person really make a difference? I believe so.

This next story is poignant to me because the people involved believed enough in the intelligence and emotions of animals to ask me to be their communicator. Yet when it was conveyed to them exactly what the problem was, and how to fix it, they immediately dismissed the idea, not even giving it a try, and this is the only reason that I include the following story. ❧

Plattie

"I won't have any more babies,
because they always take them all away!"

Defiant she was, and her sadness over this issue ran deep...

A beautiful silvery white sow, Plattie lived on a small breeding farm along the West Coast. Her human, a breeder of potbellied pigs, had acquired Plattie in the hopes that she would produce some fine pet-quality piglets as beautiful as she: however, it was not working out very well. For months the breeders tried to get Plattie bred, and although the boar was more than willing, for some reason she would not take, even though she had successful farrowings in the past. So I was asked to communicate with her to find out what was wrong.

The first time I tuned in to to her, she conveyed a deep sadness. She refused to get pregnant, she shared, because they always took her babies away. Plattie took great pride in her piglets and her own mothering abilities. "I love to watch them, teach them and see them grow. I have fine piglets, but people always take them all away." Now, she would simply not allow herself to become pregnant. She couldn't bear having one more taken away from her.

I asked her human family if they had a young pig that they could give to Plattie. One that she could finish raising and keep for her own as a companion. This seemed to me an easy way to try to corroborate the story I was getting, maybe leading to a happy, contented sow whose nurturing instincts opened her up for pregnancy once again. But the answer was "No." As a breeding farm, they said couldn't spare a saleable pig just to be Plattie's baby.

One day after a long time without word from the breeder, I received an e-mail announcing a sad development at their farm. It seems Plattie had become less and less social and dangerously aggressive. One day she charged a child who was quickly scooped up and deposited in a safe area away from the pig's pens. The next day Plattie went berserk. She was put down by the neighbor who was summoned. One shot to the head had instantly ended her suffering and grief.

Her human told me she spoke with Plattie during her euthanasia, telling her that it was going to be okay. As I read, my attention instantly went to Plattie, and it appeared to me that she had crossed over in full consciousness, albeit with a heavy heart. Once there, she lay down to sleep. As the scene played out before me I just sat there for a minute, watching her rest, before my mind's interruptive thoughts brought me back to the computer screen before me.

The e-mail went on to say that Plattie had gone berserk when piglets were being removed from the pen for a simple trip to the vet. Even though they were not babies of her own, Plattie obviously could not endure yet one more piglet being taken away. What I had conveyed to the breeder a year or so before, about giving Plattie a baby of her own to keep as a way to lessen her grief over lost piglets in the past, now came as validation to me that this might have made a difference in her life. It would have been such a small price to pay for an animal whose humans expected her to produce money for them.

The letter ended with a request from her breeder for any word that I might get from Plattie about what had happened. If I connected with her, would I tell Plattie for her that she was sorry?

I wrote back my condolences and told her that I would listen, then let it go at that. As I turned off the computer, I turned my attention once again to the peaceful picture of Plattie sleeping and added warm, comforting thoughts of my own. I blew a kiss toward heaven, then went about my day.

Plattie never relayed a message to her breeder after her death even though she did communicate to me. It was in her silence to them that she spoke most loudly. Although the means of her euthanasia sounds harsh, her physical ending was thankfully quite quick, and when she did wake up, she told me plainly, "I couldn't stop them from taking the babies away."

As of this writing, this has been the only time I have had sadness conveyed to me from an animal on the other side of life. The sadness wasn't the deep, pervading kind that she had endured while here. It seemed to be a sadness for the humans who could not see, beyond their own personal agendas, another being crying out to them in need. For this, Plattie asked that I not convey any part of our brief communication. They had ignored her grief and sadness, and now she would share with them the same.

The world is a better place when even just one human looks into the eyes of an animal and appreciates them for the sentient being that they are ～ no matter how different they are from themselves.

As an animal communicator, I hope my contribution to the world will not be from the stories animals share with me, but rather from helping another human being to realize what wisdom, grace and soul each animal on this planet is endowed with at birth. If I can help just one person become more willing to accept this truth, by listening to an animal, perhaps it will help them become more willing to listen to their neighbor and to accept their differences with respect. Maybe too, with that newfound respect, will come the willingness to give that little extra it sometimes takes to truly help a being in need. ✆

Sometimes it's our decision...

Chapter 6

Dudley

"I want you to know that we were a gift to each other ..."

The words came at a moderate pace, composed with dignity and great devotion. Dudley the horse had begun speaking to me as I typed out an invoice for Gale, whom I'd spoken with at a stable call just the night before.

Doing stable calls is one of my favorites. Several local stables use my communicating services for the horses in their charge, the owners often congregating together as a group. On this particular stable call, I spoke with 11 horses, a pony, and a cat. It was a full evening of insight and laughter, and one experience that deeply touched all who had gathered to "hear."

The group was ready when I arrived. Having been to this stable before, I quickly said hello to those I remembered, then got right to work. The fourth horse I spoke with that evening was a beautiful buckskin. Her demeanor was clever and fun, and she was always looking for a chuckle. She fit her partner, Gale, perfectly. Before the communication drew to a close, Gale stepped toward me, holding out her closed hand.

"Would you hold something for me and tell me what you get?" she asked. "I promise that I'm not setting you up."

Her eyes sparkled as I reached out my open hand, and she quietly put something onto my palm, then closed my fingers around it.

I held it for a minute or two, very happy that it didn't move, then I peeked inside. The three clumps of something looked like they'd been weathered on a beach for a long time. Reclosing my hand, I tried to assess what I was feeling.

"Please tell me anything you get," Gale said, reassuringly.

No one had ever asked me to do something like this before. As I stood quietly for another minute or so, with eyes lightly closed, an odd thing began to happen. I wasn't hearing anyone speak. No thought patterns were being offered either. Rather, a wave of emptiness completely washed over me, and I didn't understand why it would be so strong. Believing that it probably stemmed from my mounting nervousness, I dismissed it quickly and moved on to the next sensation wave that instantly followed in its wake.

"I can tell you is that it's affecting my eyes" I said, slowly opening my eyes as I spoke.

Before I could say any more, the crowd gasped, Gale's eyes filled with tears, and I stood in amazement as I watched what was happening around me.

"Those are some of the bones of my horse, Dudley," Gale replied with a sniffle. "He went blind and we had to euthanize him. I had him cremated, and those are some of the remains."

Thrilled that I had picked up on something so significant about the mystery objects held tightly in my hand, I was also now aware of a huge presence I knew was Dudley's.

"He has a very elegant feel about him, Gale," I said. "Very elegant. Was Dudley a big, elegant horse?"

"Oh, he was big and elegant. We often called him Douglas because of that!" Gale's daughter had jumped right into the conversation. Wiping the tears from her eyes then pausing briefly to blow her nose, she went on to tell me how beautiful he was.

"Dudley was a name that just did *not* do him justice."

I looked at the rest of the group, all nodding their heads in confirmation. I was struck by how this blind horse had touched so many people in this barn.

"We had to euthanize him at Cornell," Gale said, bringing my attention back around to her. As she began to tell me his story, her words became hard to hear as I drifted away off into space. Dudley was showing me pictures of his euthanasia, and I was lost in his world, unable to hear what Gale was saying. I don't know how long I stood there, totally immersed in the scene before me, but it seemed like a long time before the vision began to fade. As it did, Dudley began to speak.

Stepping forward, I put my hands around Gale's as she stood with tears streaming down her face. I vaguely remember speaking to her as Dudley spoke to me, but the exact conversation escapes me still. What I do remember is what she told me when we were done, about when she goes riding now in beautiful new places and takes along some of his ashes to scatter on the fields ∼ a fitting remembrance for a horse she knew was now free. Gale hoped Dudley was still able to see the beauty of a quiet ride in the beautiful world they had once shared.

Placing Dudley's remains back into Gale's hands, I thanked her for sharing him with me. This communication had come to a close, and a peaceful feeling swept over us all amid deep sighs. I turned to move to the next horse, who stood waiting patiently.

The next morning, Dudley's presence again filled my awareness. He had a special message for Gale, and while marvelling at his magnificent energy, I grabbed my keyboard and began to type.

> *"Where I am now, there is not time as we once perceived together. Now there is endlessness for me, and I spend it watching over you, and waiting.*
>
> *"When I was your horse, I was happy and free. When I became your memory, I became limitless in size. You gave me unbridled places to make my mark upon Earth. You carry me near and far, and you honour me with your tears.*
>
> *"I want you to know too, that what you gave me, I still have. Devotion and courage and love and joy are the gifts that are lasting, timeless, and I have mine with me. Eyes are not necessary to see gifts like these.*
>
> *"Know in your heart that I am closer than my bones. I am woven throughout time and space, I am a part of who*

you now are. Giving your love to another does not change me
in any way, rather it honours my memory, because from me
you found the courage to move on.

"Go now and touch yet another horse's life. There is
enough room in you for us all. So gather your horses, give of
yourself, laugh and be happy, be one of the herd. In this too, I
will live forever.

Dudley"

Dudley's message was mailed to Gale that very same day, but to this day I have never had a reply. Perhaps she never received it. Or perhaps no more words needed to be spoken. ✸

Samantha

"I'm pink now ⁓ my favorite colour to be!"

Sickly for the first two years of life, Samantha ultimately became the picture of health. A beautiful and elegant cat, she loved the colour pink, so when the new, pink sofa arrived, it was no surprise to find her claiming one arm of it as her own. Louise, her human mother, was glad to share this comfy spot with Sammi and the two sat there together often. Unfortunately, a problem arose soon after the sofa's arrival ⁓ Sammi's lack of bladder control. In her advancing age, she was experiencing a side effect of kidney disease, common in a cat of 17.

It became routine to check and clean Sammi's favored sofa spot, but Louise soon became frustrated. Sammi's daily accidents were one thing to deal with, but facing the inevitable was worse. Samantha's physical life was nearing completion. Louise sought out both veterinary and holistic help for Sammi, but nothing seemed to last. One day, after Samantha had a big accident on the sofa, Louise wrapped her beautiful little friend in a soft towel and took her to the vet once more. She hoped for one last miracle.

"When I got to the vet's office, and they know I'm a little emotional, he said to me, 'Louise, her kidneys are shutting down, do you want to say good-bye to her?'

"I got so nuts and depressed that I said, 'No. I can't.' Then I left her and went out through the other door, hysterical.

"They called me back in from the parking lot and said they needed to give her a shot, as it was her time. I had to sign the papers, but I never said good-bye to her."

Louise called me after returning home from Sammi's euthanasia. She was heartbroken and worried that Sammi hadn't understood why this was done to her and why there had been no good-bye.

Caught up in Louise's grief myself, at that moment I could offer her no more than a willing ear to listen. Shortly after hanging up, I got out a card and began to write a note of condolence to her. As I sat there, beginning to compose my own message, Samantha bounded into my awareness, joining in with a message of her own.

"It's *okay*, Mom!" she exclaimed, complete happiness exuding from her very presence. "It was a bit confusing when I first got there, but that lovely girl who took care of me really made me feel all warm inside."

Sammi went on to explain that she understood completely why Louise had taken her to the vet's for help. She said, too, that she was looking forward to staying right where she was for a long while.

"It's my vacation," she said, "Really, it's all right."

Samantha's last words to her grieving friend were, "I will smile at you."

Louise called two days later to thank me for her message. She confirmed that it was indeed a young girl who had attended to Sammi and told me that she'd been comforted hearing Samantha refer to this vet tech's loving care.

"When I got your note from Samantha and read how the girl at the vet's office helped her by explaining everything to her, I felt this burden just lift off of me. I was so relieved and then able to deal with it a whole different way. You made me realize that it's one thing to say that we believe in these things, but when we get the confirmation through communicators, it's a whole other thing."

This was to be just the first sudden loss for Louise. A true lover of animals, Louise had me converse with many different animals in her life each time we spoke, even those who weren't her own. Her mother's dogs, her sister's horses, Porkchop the potbellied pig, and Molly the dog next door ∼ all had a chance to speak whenever Louise called me.

Her own three cats were always listened to first, as it was her deepest desire to be sure that they had everything they needed to stay healthy and happy, even though one was already on the other side. But within weeks after Samantha's crossing, Louise called again, worried now about her charming buddy, McMurphy. ✌

McMurphy

"You must always look for happiness and smiles in every day, as this will give you many more days in which to smile again."

As a kitten, he had been rescued from under a truck in the pouring rain. A little gray tiger cat who grew into quite the wise one, McMurphy considered himself Louise's personal health consultant, always making note of her diet and what she should and shouldn't do about it.

He also loved routine. When it came to his food, in the latter part of his life, he would faithfully wake Louise up at 7 a.m. every day. Following her to the kitchen, he would watch her put breakfast food into his bowl, and then follow her back to bed without even taking a bite. It seemed he could sleep in better, just knowing that his food was in his bowl.

At 12 years old, McMurphy crossed over the Rainbow Bridge. He was euthanized to save him from suffering any longer with what had been highly suspected as colon cancer, causing him to leak from his bowels. Despite his embarrassment at having to have help from Louise to clean himself, he had remained a happy cat until the end, when he had obviously begun to suffer.

He had a dry sense of humour, which he carried on with him, along with his concern for those he left behind, particularly Louise and her remaining companion cat, Norman. McMurphy's wisdom and advice would not be curtailed by the mere loss of a physical body. Soon after he crossed over, he sent a message to be shared with his mom.

"Hello, Momma.

"This is me, McMurphy! I'm here now, with Sammi and some other cats, and I wanted you to know that I feel much better. You see, I was telling Colleen that when I looked inside my old body, I saw a terrible, nasty sight. Inside my colon I saw many little lesions which were red and mad. They had hairy edges on them and had been there for about five or six years. Some of it came from worry, which I used to do at times. And the other part was from some of the bad things in the food I ate. Man sure has a funny way of saying that they can feed your animal into health and then put all of those poisons in our food. This has been a long-term problem for the pet food industry, for at least 30 years, much longer than my nine lives.

"Now listen, I am not a leaky cat anymore. This is very much appreciated. Before I leave, I would like to ask you to listen carefully to what I have to say.

"About Norman: she is a very nice cat with a lot of mental prowess. She needs to be stimulated with talk, song and intelligent variety in her life. Listen to her about your health, okay? Oh, she likes the red ball, too.

"Be sure to give her healthful food so that she has help living to be a very old cat. She would like this. She also does not think she would like another cat, thank you. Perhaps a dog or a bunny, but she isn't sure yet.

"You should give her real meat three times per week, at least, and vegetables on a regular basis. The same for her dog, if she gets one.

"As for you: I find it necessary to me to tell you that your food choices aren't doing you a world of good either. You need to find the time to put more fresh fruit and vegetables in and take out more of the heavy foods like pasta and bread. Okay?

"Also, your personal life is a direct reflection of your inner life. This is important!!! You must always look for hap-

piness and smiles in every day, as this will give you many more days in which to smile again. I know you understand, so now I will go.

"We have things to do here, you know. Now I am going to chase that mouse that I could never catch! This is great fun for me, and it is okay ∼ it's a make-believe mouse!

"Good-bye for now, my old people mother. We will have happy times together again.

Your Irish, gray feline friend,
McMurphy"

∽

Norman

"I certainly became a very sick cat, quickly, didn't I?
You know, it's okay."

By the time the year was ending, Louise found herself having to say farewell to the last of her three feline companions, while her good friend, Paul, lay in his bed losing a battle with cancer. Having preceded Norman to the Rainbow Bridge, the only comforting thing for Louise now was to believe that Samantha and McMurphy surely awaited Norman's arrival.

In a brief conversation choked with emotion, Louise called that day to tell me of Norman's crossing. Having now acquired a sad routine with our communications ∼ her fridge bearing the results, the honoured place for the messages Sammi and McMurphy had sent her ∼ Louise's request was simple: "Can you please tell Norman I love her, and that I will be anxious to hear any message she might have for me one day, if she ever does."

There was little I could say to Louise in the moment, but I assured her that although Norman did seem asleep as we spoke, I would keep my attention on her and watch for her to awaken.

I've found that when an animal is very sick at the end, or has endured a traumatic death, the deep sleep I often find them in is one that seems to be healing to the soul. For Norman this was understandable because they had suspected she suffered from feline leukemia, a common, chronic, debilitating disease in cats these days. Hers must have become active again after McMurphy's crossing, perhaps triggered out of remission by her grief. Whatever the cause, the end result was the same, Norman slipped into a bad way, fast, and as her disease progressed quickly, Louise was unaware that she was suffering anything other than grief.

Norman was a funny girl. She never had volumes to say the way McMurphy and Sammi always did when we spoke, but she always had a way of finding humour in everyday things, imparting them in a way that always made me laugh. As I thought of her each day, while waiting for her to awaken, I wondered how much of that humour she would still convey. It wasn't too long before I had my answer.

"Hello Norman, it's me, Colleen. How are you feeling?"

Norman just looked at me, and I could sense a sly grin beginning to form on her face. In an instant she was gone, scurrying off to a place I couldn't see. But even though she left my senses, I could feel a block of thought forming in her wake, and I knew that words were about to come flying back at me. Quickly I regretted putting my purse into my carry-on bag, which was stored in the compartment above my seat. Though I lacked a tape recorder, or even a pen and piece of paper in hand, as the plane's engines roared for takeoff, Norman roared into a message for Louise.

> "Hello Mother. It's me, Norman, and I've got a lot to tell you about this place.
>
> "First of all, what's the big idea having Colleen keep track of me here? I knew she was watching me, but I snuck away when she had no pen.
>
> "There were many things for me to do when I woke up here. Oh, and remember, put this on the fridge. It's going to be good!
>
> "I certainly became a very sick cat quickly, didn't I? You know, it's okay. I thought you needed some big changes so when I was sad, I just said, 'Norman, old girl, let it go.'
>
> "McMurphy showed me a picture of you clearing away all of the old, worn-out garments in your life and I knew that

you wore me as well. This was good! Do not misunderstand what I am saying here, so if you need a break to compose yourself, please take one now and come back.

"Okay, like I was saying … I had those little bugs (cells) in me, you know, and when Sammi left, a couple of them woke up because I missed her. I even missed the big bad spots on the sofa that she used to make. (She really is a pink cat now, you know?) But I got better.

"Then McMurphy decided it was time for him to step out, too. Poor guy. It was no fun for him being embarrassed like that every day.

"Remember tail wiping?" she now began to whisper, "He really loved how you talked softly when you helped him with that." And for a moment, I lost Norman in this memory she was sharing. For this I was grateful, because the cabin's "Fasten Seatbelts" lights had just been turned off, so I jumped from my seat to retrieve a pen and pad.

"When he was gone," she resumed, "I didn't think I would mind the quiet, but those bugs in me got very loud. So, McMurphy said to me, 'Listen Norman, you might want to think about coming here with us. Momma can get along fine, and once her friend Paul is here too, then she'll not have any-more illness to think about, except maybe her own, unless she gets a grip and gets really happy again. It doesn't have to be loud for a long time Norman. Just go'!"

I thought back to how Louise had called not long before Norman crossed over. She'd been worried about her after McMurphy's death, and although his message had clearly stated that Norman would not like another cat, Louise thought that perhaps this was what Norman really did need. A friend, to spur her into action again, and get her to come out of the basement she'd been refusing to leave.

A friend had talked to Louise about a lovely stray cat that really needed a home. It was an orange girl, a colour that Norman had liked, so Louise brought her home and named her a name that one of the cats

had suggested. As I struggled to remember her name, Norman brought
my attention back to her, and she was gracious enough not to be an-
noyed at my wandering thoughts.

> *"So I thought about it for a while there in my dark
> yellow place (basement) and when you brought home Orang-
> el-opy I thought, 'Okay, this is good. But is she sitting on Mom's
> lap while I'm thinking about things?'*
>
> *"It wasn't a good time to get into a new feline ~ even
> if she was my present. I should have said right then, 'Okay,
> I'm leaving. No bunny. No Norman ...' I'm only kidding. I
> just thought that now's a good time to leave because I didn't
> want it to take forever, like Paul, and it very well could have.*
>
> *"The doctor was very nice to me and told me that you
> wanted me to get well, but you were afraid that I couldn't, and
> what would you do?*
>
> *"She said to me, 'It's okay Norman, you can go. I'll
> explain it.'*
>
> *"So I did. On my own! And it was good to get out of
> those spots.*
>
> *"Yep, slept for about two to three weeks, but it was
> more like a nap. Didn't want to talk to Colleen. It was too
> much effort. I was really tired and I didn't expect that. But
> when she flew away I laughed and said, 'Oh this will get her,
> no plane has tape recorders with lunch!' So I took off while she
> watched me run by.*
>
> *"Haven't been back home since. Been busy and have
> lots to do. Sammi is going to wait for you, she says. She
> expects to be here a long time.*
>
> *"McMurphy has lots to show me, but is thinking of
> taking on an adventure in the real world. I will be staying
> here, as I don't know what I want to do yet.*
>
> *"Have you thought about a parrot for a friend? You
> do like to talk a lot.*
>
> *"Maybe a cat isn't a good idea because they won't be*

like us guys. No matter what, just look first and give them the
right name," she said, alluding to her own hasty naming.
　　"Bye now, Mother ～ I've got balls to chase and birds
to watch. I'm a good cat now and you helped me be that.
Sickness is just a journey we sometimes choose to take.
　　"Remember that. Remember me.

　　Your good friend always,
　　Norman ～ Your happy little girl"

When I interviewed Louise for this book, I asked her if she would share with me what animal communicating has meant to her. The reply came without hesitation.

"When I first spoke with you, when my kitty cats were all still here, you had never met me or been in my home yet you were saying things that left me awed. In that very first conversation we had, you suddenly said that Sammi said, 'Don't sit there, I'll be right back,' and at the same time you were saying this, I watched Samantha hop down and walk off. It freaked me out. It made me feel so much closer to my animals and feel a deeper love than I ever had. I thought to myself, Oh my God, these animals are so real and connected on a level that I didn't know. It's like I sensed it before, but it had so much more meaning when I realized that they truly understood what I was saying to them. I told my friend Rita, that I couldn't thank her enough for telling me about you.

"So when I got the first note, from you and Samantha, it was a gift because then I knew that she really understood why I took her to the vet and that she didn't feel hurt that I had left her. So my Sammi was the first to go. Her message was my first real introduction to being able to talk with animals on the other side. What a godsend."

Louise is a very special person to me. Within 18 months, she lost all three of her cats; the dog next door, Molly, whom she walked almost every day; and her boyfriend, Paul. I couldn't imagine what kind of basket case I would have been had all of these things happened to me, and within such a short period of time, too.

As awed as Louise had confessed to having been, regarding my ability to communicate with animals, I have been equally awed by her, a woman who has lost so many loves in her life, yet still calls me to this day, to speak and laugh with animals that still are not her own.

Like me, Louise has found a richness in life that the animals provide through communication. And I have now found a richness in the spirit of humans like Louise, who find comfort in a message from an animal friend in heaven, and then translate it into an even deeper love for the ones who are still here to speak.

I believe Louise is a tribute to the animals she loves, because she is *always* ready to listen, even if she believes they may ask her to say good-bye.

I am honoured that she calls me her friend. ✎

Molly

"You talked to me, I heard you.
*I **always** hear my mom,*
and when I go to heaven first,
I will listen for your songs..."

Golden retrievers are a very special breed of dog, and Molly was no exception. She lived with her human mom, Ellen, and a Border Collie named Schubert, who was twice Molly's age and in poor health. Together they lived in a house filled with music and love for each other.

When Ellen called me, it was for a second opinion animal communication. Smiling at the prospect of what this consult might reveal, compared to a fellow communicator's word, I put my attention onto Molly and asked Ellen where she'd like to begin.

Ellen began by telling me that Molly, although only seven years old, had recently been diagnosed with an inoperable brain tumour on the right side of her brain. Advised by her veterinarian that a conventional treatment with steroids could prove helpful, Ellen took to heart the warning that it would only do so for a limited time.

The communicator before me had felt Molly was saying that she wanted to give this route a try. I was beginning to receive something similar, but with a little twist.

"She says she will try, if you want her to, Ellen," I said. "But she is embarrassed at her lack of body control."

Molly showed me pictures of her constant circling, something I knew was indicative of a brain tumour. She also conveyed that she didn't mind going to Cornell, an option that Ellen said she'd considered when her vet had offered her the referral.

Ellen also told me that if they did indeed go, she may have to leave Molly there for a day or two. Whatever happened, she would base her decision on what the prognosis for this treatment would be.

"I just want to be with my mom," Molly said in closing. "I want her to sing to me."

Ellen laughed and commented on how she never thought her singing meant that much to the dogs, but with this said, she would be sure to indulge Molly more. We left our conversation with Ellen feeling just a little better about their sad state of affairs, and I hung up the phone feeling a little undone.

Long after our conversation ended, Molly still hung around. It just felt like there was something else she wanted to say. Sitting at the keyboard, I invited her to join me again, and slowly but surely Molly conveyed her message. It took her a while to get it all out, and I assumed it was because the tumour interfered with her thoughts. But her diligence paid off, and the poem below is what Molly really wanted to say to her mom that day.

"You talked to me, I heard you.
I always hear my mom,
and when I go to heaven first,
I will listen for your songs.

"They'll float across the sun-swept sky
and they'll blend with who I am.
Remember we will never die,
so please do not think of me and cry.

"I am Molly, then and now.
You are Mom, my friend.
We'll see each other one day soon,
because death is not an end."

A few weeks later, I received a letter from Ellen. In it she told me of Molly's passing and how they'd spent their last days together.

"I didn't realize that my singing made Molly happy," she wrote. "When I brought her home from Cornell, I sang to her a lot, making up Molly-words to my favorite Schubert lullaby. It was a comfort to the both of us."

Ellen went on to tell me that she and Molly had driven to Cornell for a second opinion, knowing euthanasia might be the most humane way of dealing with Molly's quickly deteriorating condition. She also said that when they got into the car to go, she had decided to leave the decision of what to do up to Molly.

"I walked her to the car and opened the back door. She jumped right in all by herself," Ellen said. "So I took that as my cue to bring her home, supplied with Cortisone tablets, instead of putting her to sleep. All week I sang to her, and gave her the best food and supplements.

"On Thursday, your letter with Molly's poem came," Ellen continued in her note. "It made me cry. That evening she took a turn for the worse, and I realized the tumour was making her life impossible. Your letter and her poem gave me the courage to make the decision to call the vet in the morning and have her put to sleep.

"While a friend took Schubert on a walk, I said good-bye to Molly in my back yard, in a sunny spot on the grass under a tree. It was very sad, but I could not have hoped for her ending to have been nicer ~ out in the yard where she had once chased frisbees and squirrels, dug holes, chewed on sticks and run around with Schubert."

Ellen finished by telling me how loved Molly had been by the neighborhood children and her piano students, who missed her smiling golden face already. She also wrote that Schubert had made a great recovery, and I smiled with relief to know that Ellen wouldn't be calling me again, too soon, facing the same dilemma with him.

It's hard enough to lose a beloved companion, I thought to myself. It just seems cruel, when you have more than one, to lose them all in short succession.

"The poem Molly gave you is a great comfort to me. I plan to frame it, along with a photo of her," Ellen said in closing, and I could almost picture the revered place Ellen might hang this memento.

Sitting back in my chair I smiled again. What a wonder it is for me each time I am honoured to see how the animals are able to comfort us, even while facing their own physical demise.

Once more I was thankful to have known yet one more "lowly animal" who spoke with simple words of simple pleasures, coupled with tremendous insight.

"If only more humans could awaken one day to find themselves in such a state of understanding," I whispered to my office walls… If only humans could aspire to such wisdom and grace. ⟷

Sometimes it's their decision...

Chapter 7

Freeway

Referring to himself as a pizza-loving junkyard dog, Freeway and my good friend, Joyce, had been companions for 13 years ...

"Excuse me, but didn't you forget something?"

An old dog who had suffered three probable strokes during the last few years, one day Freeway decided he really wanted tomatoes in his diet. Although a seemingly odd request for a dog, Joyce was quick to indulge him with the juicy red fruit, his newfound dietary desire. By the spring of 1995, as Joyce watched her old friend's health decline, I asked Freeway if he was ready to leave his body yet. He told me he didn't think so, that he'd been thinking he'd just wait around until the next fall when the tomatoes were ready in the garden again.

Summer days passed, and as autumn turned to winter, leaving the garden's tomato vines cold and bare, Freeway decided he now wanted tomato sauce on his dinner each night. Although the store-bought kind was okay, he really enjoyed the sauce Joyce had made that fall. And, if in the dinnertime haste she forgot to add it to his bowl, he would stand there, wobbling a little from his latest stroke, looking up patiently, saying, "Excuse me, but didn't you forget something?"

Once the sauce was added, he would go right to it, eating all of his dinner and happily cleaning his bowl. On special occasions, like holidays and the sort, Freeway would dine upon the fresh hot-house variety, although they first needed to be left on the counter to warm up.

After Thanksgiving, Joyce called to tell me that she had been read-ing a natural health magazine and found the most incredible thing and couldn't wait to share it with me. It was an article on what to eat now to avoid certain diseases in the future, and we both were amazed at what it said: Strokes ∼ Tomatoes!

We believe that Freeway had one more stroke in mid-December. Within 24 hours, his health and his ability to stand or void voluntarily, declined rapidly. He started sleeping all the time, and when communi-cating with him I got a confused, muddled feeling, as if he could no longer focus or think clearly. He seemed to be out of his body more than in it.

On Christmas Day, Freeway started trembling and losing body heat. Unable to stand, he was covered up and sent warm, loving pictures by his family that it was okay to go. The day after, I received one message from him, "I need help. I am trying to go, but it doesn't work right." He also asked that Daddy go with him in the car.

On December 27, Freeway's lifelong veterinarian helped him cross over to the other side of life. Two days later I had received only one message from him, "I'm here!" He then conveyed that he was enjoying a long-deserved, restful sleep.

At 2:50 p.m. on Thursday, January 4, 1996, while at my desk, I suddenly saw Freeway before my eyes, in his "light body." I saw him wake up, stand, and start mogging on home! He looked great, about the way he did four years earlier, before his first stroke. He said nothing.

I grabbed the phone to call Joyce, only to find she was not at her desk. At 3:30 p.m. I tried again, but no Joyce. Disappointed at not reaching her, I hung up and my day ended without another chance to call her.

Early the next morning, I called Joyce to make arrangements to pick up feed for a client, telling her I hoped to get there before she left for work. When I pulled into the driveway, I saw that her car was already gone, but for some reason I still couldn't take my eyes off of the house. At first glance, no one seemed to be there, except for Freeway. Standing on the sofa behind the picture window, he was shouting to me, "I'm home! I'm home now!'"

Surprised, yet elated, I closed my eyes, smiled the biggest smile, and thanked him for welcoming me again with his great news. Just after lunch I called Joyce, to tell her the whole story. I barely gave her a chance to say hello before blurting out about trying to call her at 3 p.m. the day before, when my first vision of Freeway occurred, and what I had experienced in her driveway that morning.

"Oh, you're just who I needed to talk to, Colleen," she told me, after pausing for a moment. "At exactly 2:53 p.m. yesterday, I was walking across the parking lot to my car after leaving the pet cemetery office. I had just picked up Freeway's ashes to bring them home."

Freeway graces their home with his presence once again. He told me he had no immediate plans yet for moving on, and how wonderful it is that Daddy doesn't trip over him anymore because now he has an invisible body. He doesn't even have to get up and move. And the last thing that Freeway conveyed that day, was that he just might hang around a while ∿ to see how the tomatoes look that summer.

Euthanasia is probably one of the hardest decisions a pet owner will ever make on behalf of their animals.. Even if we believe ending the pain and suffering of a beloved animal friend, who has no hope of recovering, is the kindest thing to do, we must also deal with our own grief at the same time. For many humans left behind, this grief is compounded by the fear that their animal friend may have been angry at them for letting this happen, for ending their life. In Freeway's case, helping him to cross over was not only a blessing, but a request he made himself. This made the road to the vet's slightly easier for Joyce to travel that day.

"Knowing they are still alive and well, and doing the things they used to do, but without pain, has helped me to get through these kinds of losses. I only grieve their physical absence, because I know they are often still here with me for a time. I just can't see them like I used to," she told me.

It is that physical loss that I, too, have found so hard to get used to. Not having that faithful friend there to greet you when you come home from a long day at work, or to share an afternoon nap with on a blustery, gray day, leaves many with an aching heart that seems irreparable at times. Feedback from my clients has shown me that their belief in an animal's afterlife can be a shining beacon to them in an otherwise gloomy period. They still cry, grieve and feel lost without their furry or feathered companion, but it is not the total devastation that many suffer from, and from which some never recover.

Feeling responsible for another's death must truly be a hard burden to bear and that is why I found Freeway's story so beautiful. It was the first instance, in my earlier work, in which I had an animal ask for help in crossing over. Since then I have heard others utter this same request, each for a different reason, and each as equally captivating. ✧

Randolph

"Okay, here I am.
How come you left me sprawled out under the desk?
Were you happy that I ran away? I ran here as fast as I could.
That's what all the thinking was about ⁓ what I was doing
before I left."

Randolph was a long-haired, smoky-coloured, rough-and-tumble, city-born cat when I first met him, but he lived the last few years of his nine lives in a beautiful country setting. After nine years of apartment living, the move to the country would be an exciting event for Kathy. Now she would own her own small farm, complete with indoor and outdoor cat facilities, and all of the urban cats she was tending to were welcome to come along, if they wished.

"I want the cats to know that I'm leaving on Saturday. I'm more than happy to take anyone who'd like to come with me, but they have to tell me now," she explained to both me and the cats in a conversation she had scheduled a week before the move.

"I know that Angelica and everyone else indoors will be happy to have a nice big house to live in, but I don't want to impose my new abode on the outdoor cats I've been feeding," she told me. "They need to know that they have a choice, but once I leave, with or without them, they can't change their mind."

Kathy gave me the name of each outdoor cat, as she knew them by, and one by one we spoke to each, explaining the situation and asking for their response.

Randolph was quick to answer that he'd love to become a leisurely country cat, but in actuality, I believe he just wanted to reap the rewards that fat country mice would provide him. When moving day arrived, Kathy loaded seven cats into her car, and they left city living behind them.

Randolph had always been a bruiser, coming home with fur missing, his skin gashed open. Once in the country, his lifestyle mellowed some, but he would still arrive home at times looking as if he'd suffered the losing end of a cat squabble.

One day, years after the move, I answered the phone to find Kathy on the other end of the line, near hysteria. The irresponsible neighbors down the road had again let their pack of dogs run loose, and she'd come home from work to find one of her pet ducks, Jack, dead in her driveway. After wandering around in shock, looking for Jack's mate, Esmé, she found her hiding in the garage, along with some very traumatized cats. Randolph was one of them, having obviously witnessed the gruesome event.

Over the next few weeks, everyone slowly recovered from the vicious dog attack, except Randolph, who appeared to be doing a lot of thinking when inside. Although he was now a very old age, and sporting a slightly smaller waistline, Randolph's whole demeanor deteriorated rapidly. Weight began to fall off steadily, and when let outdoors, he refused to leave the back porch. Kathy would find him there, crying and quivering with fear. It seemed he could not shake off what horrors he had seen. Within a few more days, he passed away.

Kathy was getting ready for work the morning she found Randolph's body stretched out under the desk in her library. Reaching down to pat her friend, she quickly realized he was not sleeping. Deeply saddened that she hadn't been able to help him overcome his last battle wounds ∼ the ones in his heart ∼ she left him laying there. She would need to ready his grave in the small section of the farm which had been dedicated as the animals' memorial spot. Randolph knew this spot from when his longtime friend Angelica had been laid to rest there. Afterwards, she called to tell me of Randolph's passing and asked if I would think of him in the next few days. I was pleased to do so. A few days later, Randolph had much to say. As his first thoughts came blasting through my mind, I dashed to my computer, not wanting to miss a word.

"So this is how it happened," Randolph said, as his words leapt from him to me. " I got up one morning and I decided that I was pretty much done with the things I had to do. After all, I'd been working on them for a long time. I managed nicely too," he continued. "Even if it didn't always look like I had. By the way, thank you for always helping my fur to grow back. It's embarrassing to be seen without it in spots. Makes you look like a loser or something. In actuality, though, it represented great feats of strength and power against a formidable foe.

"Now I'm here and I've been awake the whole time. I know because I never stopped hearing Angelica calling to me. 'Come On old cat! It's time to be the Big Cheese!'

"She says that because you do special things for our bodies when we leave them. I was always impressed with that when I was there. So, I'm expecting great fanfare from you in a few days. You know what that means? A party! Cheese and other good food for all!

"So here I am without much to do. I know I can do anything I want, but I think I'll ponder that for a while. After all, I was pretty busy back there.

"Did you know that you look all fuzzy now?" the cat asked, and he showed me how he was seeing Kathy, as through a mist. It was the ultimate in soft-focus, I thought.

"And I'm going to stay here just a while before I try something else. No, I'm not coming back there now. I'm trying something different, but I don't know what yet.

"I'm going. Angelica is going to show me how to jump really high now. It's a fun thing to do and I know I'll land on my feet.

"Thank you for my house and food. Thank you for

petting me and always loving my hairless spots. Thank you for giving me cheese and warm water whenever I asked, and thank you for asking me what I thought about things. I appreciate that a lot, and I will always remember it.

"*And don't worry, I'll still tell you about things here, because I know how this works now. You still keep talking to us even after our bodies wear out. That's pretty nice. I think I'll brag about that to some cats up here. I won't get a bad reputation either because I'll do it in a nice way. Something like: 'Hey, did you know that I still talk to my girl? What, you can't do that?'*

"*I suppose it will mean a job for me, teaching these cats how to do it with the people they might still want to talk to.*

"*Geesh, and just when I thought I'd get a vacation.*

Your favorite cat,
Randolph"

Kathy and I have spoken to him a few times in the years since he crossed over. I don't recall him having much to say, other than offering a sentence or two of his worldly advice.

Kathy's memorial spot at the farm has grown some in size, but the memories of each friend gone are far larger than the small piece of earth their physical bodies rest in.

On a side note, you may like to know that Randolph has joined me here as I've worked on his story for you to read. He has even brought along his old friend Harvey, his good friend from his days of living in the city. I never knew Harvey because he had crossed over before Kathy and I ever met.

They're both sitting here, to my right, on top of my scanner. Neither one looking worse for wear, and with all fur apparently intact. Randolph is explaining to Harvey how you talk to the people you knew, so that they will hear you all the way from heaven.

"HEY!" he shouts at me, then looks back at his friend.

Harvey merely continues to clean his creamy orange face with a paw. It seems Randolph needs to work more on his communication skills. Or perhaps he needs to find a buddy who really cares. ✞

Bela

"I don't mind going. It doesn't scare me at all. I can stay for a while, if you like, but not if I get embarrassing."

The pictures Bela showed me were of the accident he'd had a few days before, the day he had found a weak spot in his pigpen's fencing and decided to slip out for a walk on the wild side. During my communication with Bela, he showed me clearly how he had wandered down the field, then up toward the road, having hoofed it quite a ways from home.

Images flowed freely through my mind. Bela communicated quite well with pictures, and I was glad to be able to see such detail, feeling as if I were there myself, looking out through his eyes. No sooner had I begun to realize this fact than a car came whizzing by me. Suddenly everything in this vision Bela shared went topsy-turvy.

At a small farm in Arkansas, about 10 miles from their house, Kim and Jan lovingly governed a sanctuary for many rescued pet pigs. The pigs had a large area where the main herd lived, with some smaller, private pens for those individuals who either needed or preferred to live by themselves, alongside the others. Bela had not required privacy, so he spent his days with his best buddy, Boaris, in the main herd.

"At the time when all this happened, every now and then our pigs would break out, then go visit the big pig down the road, whom we eventually renamed Miss Mary. Whenever anybody was missing, we could usually find them conversing with her," Jan wrote, after I asked her to help me recreate Bela's story.

"We always went down, both morning and evening, to feed and check on the pigs, but we didn't count the entire herd every single time. So, when Bela escaped, we didn't know he was missing until our neighbor called," she went on.

"Your pig is in our creekbed and our pig is with him," the neighbor said.

So, on the day in question, Bela had acted alone. No one else seemed to have found the weak spot in the fence through which he had slipped, before trotting off on his own, presumably to head on down the way to converse with their friend, Miss Mary.

Pig's snouts are almost always to the ground in search of something to eat or to entertain themselves with. Because of this, containing them can be a bigger chore than one might think. With their powerful necks, they can heave a weak fence easily, or keep testing a stronger one until it finally gives in. Although Kim's and Jan's fencing had been constructed especially for their pigs, it did not give them any solace to know they had done nothing wrong. The end result was the same: Bela had gotten out, and they found him terribly wounded.

Bela indicated to me that he had *not* been hit by the car that whizzed by in the pictures of his accident he'd first shared with me. Rather it had startled him, as it had me. Then jumping in fright, he had rolled down the embankment on the side of the road. Over and over and over he went, with no stopping in sight.

Considering that pigs do *not* like to be upside down, I knew this was a big event in his life ⁓ so much so, that it left his hind legs paralyzed.

"We went down to the neighbor's and found Bela sitting in the creekbed unable to move his back legs, his back broken in the fall," Kim said. "Meanwhile, Miss Mary picked up on his distress, via 'pig radar,' and broke out of her pen."

Kim added that this was the first time Miss Mary had ever done this. And after she broke out, she went to Bela's side and sat with him for what they later found had been three days, until he was found. According to the neighbors, Miss Mary's owners at the time, Miss Mary could only be persuaded back into her pen once Kim and Jan were on their way to rescue Bela.

The vet did not have a good prognosis for Bela and offered the kind advice of euthanasia. But Kim and Jan wanted to wait a bit longer. They wanted time to ask Bela what he wanted to do. That is when they called me.

Immediately I was struck with the light-hearted, easy-going feeling of this pig and his remarkable indifference toward his injuries. If I hadn't been told so already, I don't know whether I would have picked up on his injuries and the vet's grim prognosis. Happiness exuded from Bela, and he was eager to communicate more.

"Bring me more red apples, cut in four pieces," he said.

"He is enjoying all of the attention you're giving him," I replied, as I dove into myself and got really in tune with his "feeling."

"He's showing me the extra treats you are giving him to get him to move about."

Chuckling to myself, I knew this was always a good approach with a pig.

"We don't want to go with the vet's recommendation unless Bela wants it that way," Jan said. "We've been thinking that maybe we could have one of those carts built for him, like dogs use, and we could place his hind end onto it so he could pull himself around."

Bela however, instantly indicated that he did not want a cart strapped to his rump and was incredulous that a dog would be willing to go this route. Despite reassurances to the contrary, this dignified pig feared he would just look too stupid, so the idea was scratched.

I sympathized with the women, who wanted only to help their little pal, as they searched in vain to find a way for Bela to have a quality life, no matter how long that life might be. And they were very worried about him injuring himself further while dragging himself around on the ground.

"He has to keep moving about, but because he doesn't have feeling in his back end, first he'll drag off his bristles, and then his skin," Kim said. "His potbelly will get sore too, from dribbling urine. Since he doesn't want a cart, I don't know how we'll keep a sore clean."

As they related all of their concerns to me, Bela interjected here and there, and in the end, he requested that he not be allowed to get into that kind of state.

Again, he assured us that if and when such things did happen, he would want to go, because death did not frighten him at all. I was also sure he would clearly let them know, if and when, that time had arrived. They would not have to question themselves.

"If I can't go on my own, *then* could you get me some help?" he asked. "And will you stay with me while I leave?"

These were hard words to hear, but as we all took deep breaths, Bela was assured that his requests would certainly be met.

"And could I have a soft, blue blankie?" he asked in one final request.

It was delivered to him within a few hours.

A few days later, Bela became depressed and did not want to move around, even for treats. Kim and Jan called again, and Bela told them that it was alright if they wanted to call the vet now.

Bela also requested that he be buried with his blue blankie.

"I don't mean to be selfish," he said, "but a pig's blankie is a very personal thing."

"Bela came to a very peaceful end," Kim wrote, "and he was buried in our yard with his blue blankie, as requested. We also decided that Miss Mary shouldn't be rewarded for her epic act of heroism by ending up in someone's frying pan, so we entered into a complicated series of negotiations for her life. In what we still call 'The Jimmy Hoffa Deal,' we agreed to trade Miss Mary for an already-wrapped pig of similar size."

The women agreed that this was a rather morbid-sounding deal indeed. The "already-wrapped" pig had gone to slaughter before the trade was even considered or discussed, but with this offer in hand, now Miss Mary would not endure the same fate.

They called again to speak with Miss Mary, both to inform her of the pardon she had received on their behalf, and also to tell her that they were coming for her.

"I will be watching for you," she told them.

And, sure enough, when Kim and Jan first caught sight of her as they walked across the field, taking the same route Bela probably had, Miss Mary was seen sitting by the fence at the back of her pen, patiently waiting for them to take her home.

The fence was broken down and Miss Mary emerged with what seemed a smile upon her face. Together they walked back across the open fields, to the farm where all of the little potbelly pigs lived.

"I love these little pigs," she said upon entering her new pig yard. "I will be good to them," she added. And she has been.

Later that same year, Kim and Jan were able to construct special barns and a feeding area at their own home. Then they moved all of the pigs to their house so they could now all be close to each other. It was a non-traumatic move for the pigs, and their new home hosts acres of pastures and woods in which the pigs spend their days grazing, sunning and rooting.

Just before this move, a good friend of Kim's and Jan's, and especially the pigs, had died. For a few years, Bill had often taken care of the pigs' twice-a-day feedings, and on those days he would tell everyone in town that he had to go "take care of all his kids." At his funeral he was buried with a small stuffed baby pig and the keys to the gate at the pigs' farm.

Shortly after Bill's death and before I had been told who Bill was, Bela appeared in a conversation that Kim and Jan were having with the herd. Bela wondered about the toy Bill had arrived with. It was obvious to us that when Bill had arrived in heaven, Bela was there to greet him.

Kim and Jan explained to Bela that they sent him with a little pig because he had loved him and his herd so dearly while here.

Bela agreed, and then said, "But you needn't send the keys, because there are no locked gates where we are."

"Miss Mary is still here," Kim wrote, "happily in charge of all the little pigs. She is still cuddling up nightly with Boaris, Bela's best friend in life.

"And I imagine Bill and Bela are off drinking coke together some-where, in that place with no locked gates. But, I'd be very surprised if Bill gets to share the soft blue blankie."

And as I finished reading Kim's letter, I was thankful for the help she gave me in recreating Bela's story, the part I didn't know before our first conversation. Sitting back in my chair, I thought about how this story had many twists and turns, but in the end, it was really just one big story with one beautiful message ⌒ we all belong to each other, in a life which always goes on. ⬧

Lucky

"I've learned a lot being with you.
I learned about love and happiness and being your friend."

Having the misfortune of being left on the side of the road by the driver of the car which had just hit her and sped off, Lucky had the good fortune of Joan driving right behind. Joan stopped and ran to Lucky's side. Small in stature but big in heart, Joan scooped up the dog's broken body despite the fact that this dog looked like a wolf with German Shepherd markings. Carefully she transported her to the vet, where her injuries were tended to quickly. No doubt, Joan had saved Lucky's life ∽ hence her new name.

When I first met Joan it was in a consult with both of her dogs. She wanted to know how Shera and Lucky were doing together. It seemed there was some undesirable behavior going on, and Shera began to tell of her distaste for the new addition to their household.

Joan talked about how Lucky was a bit aggressive in her patrolling of the yard's perimeter, and she wanted Lucky to know that there was no need to look for trouble, that they lived in a very peaceful place. Joan also wanted Lucky to know that Shera had lived there first and that she should not be mean to her.

We all discussed ideas that could hopefully change the disrupted home back into a loving, peaceful abode, and Shera hesitantly agreed to allow Lucky to live at her house. Joan took note of the tone of the conversation between the dogs, and of Lucky's comment about her previous owner, who had called her "Wolf." It did seem appropriate. Confident that this was all we could accomplish at this time, I thanked the dogs for speaking with me, and we ended our conversation.

Later that year, I met Joan again when she attended an introductory animal communication workshop I held. At the end of the seminar, everyone left feeling they had indeed communicated with an animal that day, and all were eager to go home to put the new techniques they learned to use with their own companion animals.

I didn't hear from Joan again for a whole year. When she called to make another appointment, it was with a sadness in her voice. Things had not been going very well. The aggression had improved some, but then relapsed. She contemplated giving Lucky away to a family in which she would be an only dog, but then Lucky's health took a turn for the worse.

Although she had pretty much recovered from her injuries sustained when she was hit by the car, she now was suffering from a terminal illness. Her body was giving out on her, and Shera was even more intent on letting Lucky know that she was not welcome in her home. As this caused many vicious fights to ensue, Joan didn't know what to do. She didn't think it would be fair to a new family to get a dog with a terrible health problem. On top of that, she didn't think that Lucky would be happy going to a new home ∼ especially now that she was quite sick. Should she euthanize her?

Our conversation that day centered on what Lucky wanted to do. With the situation of the frequent fights and discord in their home, Lucky understood that it was very hard for Joan to endure this kind of behavior, not to mention that it was hard on Lucky physically with her body in the sad shape it was in.

Lucky thought about going to a new home and whether that would be desirable to her, but after a short while, she plainly told me that this was not the course she would like to take. She would rather be helped over to the next realm now, before her body deteriorated to an embarrassing state, than to go live with people she didn't belong to. This was her home, and she wanted to stay here until it was time for her to cross over. She wasn't afraid to die, but she was afraid to do it in the new surroundings of another home. It was obvious that she felt she belonged with Joan, for however long that may be.

Joan left our conversation feeling more confident that euthanizing Lucky would be the kindest thing to do. She said that she would tend to it at the week's end, giving them a few more days to spend some quality time together, and so that she could prepare Lucky for her final trip to the vet by talking everything over with her faithful friend. She also had time to talk things over with Shera, letting her know that just because Lucky was making this trip, she should not worry that she might be making it as well. Spending the time to speak with both of her dogs, helping them to understand what was about to transpire, also helped Joan deal with her own emotions.

A few weeks later, Joan called asking for an appointment with Lucky. I was confused by her request, because Lucky was immediately making herself known to me and she was exuberant and full of life. For a moment I wondered if she had come into a remission, but Joan quickly let me know that she wondered how Lucky was doing now that she had crossed over.

Lucky's conversation was full of joy, happiness and gratitude. She thanked Joan for the beautiful transition, and then she showed me how Joan had stayed with her while the vet gave her the shot. Joan agreed that she had felt at the time Lucky's transition was a very peaceful one.

Lucky went on to tell of how her first sight was of her own mother, who said to her, "Look at yourself, you're not all broken up anymore!"

Lucky appeared to be in a green place that was devoid of any other recognizable images to me, but the feeling was that of limitlessness. I felt as if I were in a warm, glowing liquid, which Lucky quickly told me was the feeling of love.

"I want to thank you for making me Lucky," she said to Joan. "You helped me when I was all broken and you loved me anyway." Lucky went on to tell Joan how fortunate she felt for having had such a wonderful experience with humans, since her beginning with humans had gone poorly.

"The last time I was a wolf, and humans were not in my world much," she said.

She showed me herself as a beautiful, big wolf, being chased off by a human wielding a weapon, and sheep were in the background. I nodded in recognition of how limited connections with humans would have been for a wolf who only sneaked in for a quick grab of lamb when needed. This time around, as a dog, she found that humans still can wield big weapons, like cars, and cause pain and suffering to her. But humans could also show her great compassion and love. She truly was grateful for these experiences.

"I've learned a lot being with you," she said. "I learned about love and happiness and being your friend. Thank you for making me your dog. I will remember, and you will see me again, but the next time I will be much bigger."

"Maybe a horse, Lucky?" Joan blurted, her enthusiasm leading me to believe this would be just fine. I smiled, admiring how size was not an issue that concerned Joan. Then I listened for Lucky's reply, which never came. There was only a feeling of joy.

Joan asked Lucky if she was happy with where they buried her. She responded immediately, saying that she didn't really care, but that if they wanted to put a memorial on the spot, she would like it to be a rock carved with a line drawing of a wolf baying at the moon.

She showed me exactly what she was thinking of, and I found myself so wishing that I had the talent to draw what I was seeing. Joan said that she would do just that for her, along with fulfilling Lucky's request for a little party, when the stone is put in place.

"Be happy in my spot," Lucky said in closing. She then turned and faded away. ☙

Sometimes we wonder why...

Chapter 8

Duchess of Pork

"I was not a pig of leisure,
but rather a pig of great importance."

In the peaceful springtime setting of beautiful Buck's County, Pennsylvania, in an old stone house built in 1734, Duchess and her brother entered the world with the wide-eyed wonderment every newborn shares. They grew and played innocently while wandering this beautiful estate, and their mother Lulabelle was always by their side. Unaware of what life ahead would bring, piglethood for these two was a special time, indeed. And, from this idyllic setting began a special story that's almost too beautiful for words ⁓ a story that would eventually touch people and pigs the world around, for many years to come. Let me begin…

"Lulabelle and I have a special relationship," Susan told me. "She is like my best friend, much like one you have from high school. I trust her with my greatest secrets and I look to her when I am needy. If you ask her, I think she will tell you that I am her best friend, too.

"When Duchess and her brother were born, I knew it would be Lulabelle's fifth litter, and her last. This alone made it very special to me.

"The day she gave birth, we spent the day together, hardly a moment apart. We laid and breathed through the labor pains together, and finally they came, just the two of them. We didn't expect too many, but we did think at least three.

"Daily care was easy with only two piglets, leaving more time for play and loving. As the weather grew warmer, the piglets would trail behind Lulabelle as she strolled about, grazing throughout the yard and just into the woods that surround the grounds. The piglets were so healthy and playful that everyone who visited the farm fell in love with them. It was one Kodak moment after another.

"The morning at Ross Mill Farm is special, and it starts just before dawn. On the floor, upon a large blanket, leaning up against the kitchen cupboards, I have my first cup of coffee with pigs on my lap. Both piglets would climb up and snuggle under my chin, one on each side. I think this was a most cherished time for Duchess and me, and I know it is my most cherished memory with these piglets."

I put Susan's letter down and enjoyed in my mind the picture Susan was painting. I had been to her estate a few times before, and I smiled at my own recollection of sitting in the same place as I tried to coax piglets onto my lap. The older pigs were almost always ready for a good scratch or tummy rub, but the piglets were often elusive, unless Susan was calling to them.

I have always envied the relationship Susan has with the many pigs who come and go from her farm. Whether it's her own pigs, their offspring, the boarding pigs who come to Piggy Camp while their families are away, or the rescued pigs that she works tirelessly for, helping them to find the safe, loving homes they each deserve, it matters not. Susan sends out a beacon of love to each pig in her charge, and they respond in kind. It's a beautiful thing to see, and as I got up from my desk to go retrieve a hot cup of tea, I thought of how fortunate I am to have such a person for my friend.

Susan's letter went on to describe how excited she was when her longtime friends, Barbara and Bob, asked her if they could adopt both piglets. The answer was yes. She knew that if they stayed on the farm with her, they wouldn't get the personal attention these special piglets deserved, so it was a blessing for Susan to know they were going to a family where they would never want for anything.

"It was an early morning flight out of Philadelphia but I still got up earlier than usual even though I had everything prepared the night before. Richard, my husband, realized this was a difficult time for me because I loved these piglets, so he quickly offered to drive them to the airport for me. As I had a last cup of coffee with my babies, Richard snapped a picture that captured a most special moment in my life. In it, I can clearly see that they loved me too. I'll treasure this picture for life.

"Don't worry," she explained to them as she put each one into their crate. "Barbara will be right there when you land at the airport." And she was.

"When we learned that Lulabelle was pregnant with her last litter, we thought about adding a female potbellied pig to our family, which already shared the wonderful companionship of Lady Lee and Lord Chapman. Then, when they were born, there were just the two of them. We knew they were a team and did not want to split them up. Little did I know, when we decided to ask for them both, how very fortunate our decision would turn out to be."

My friend Barbara had called me with news of the piglets' expected arrival. She also wanted to have a conversation with all of the pigs, before the new little ones arrived, hoping it would foster a smooth transition for all. You see pigs are herd animals, and within a herd (which can even be just two), there is *always* a herd leader. Adding new pigs to a herd can be a very stressful time, for the pigs as well as for the humans who love them. It can get brutal at times, until the herd finally recognizes one as leader. On top of this, *pigs hate change.* So, Barbara considered it polite to inform each pig about the changes to the quiet lives they had enjoyed, knowing herself what was about to take place.

First, she wanted Lady and Lord to know that these were babies coming live with them, so no rough stuff would be acceptable. Also, like themselves, they would have royal names, too. With this as a start, my work as a communicator began, and I introduced myself to the Duchess of Pork and her brother, the Duke of Earl, while acknowledging how good it was to be speaking with Lady and Lord again, too.

We all conversed back and forth as Lady, Lord, Barb and the piglets shared information about such things as when they would come; where they would sleep; how the yard would be divided (so that the young ones could get used to their new home while the older two would not have to be fully invaded by their arrival); and a big issue to pigs ∼ mealtime procedures. I remember being somewhat envious of Barb the prospect of new babies arriving that spring, but as I leaned back in my chair after hanging up the phone, I savored the relaxed atmosphere my own herd had achieved. As I watched Clover and Harry sleeping in the kitchen, outside my office door, I smiled. Part of me was envious no longer, knowing what lay ahead for my friends who were about to have disrupted their own peaceable kingdom.

Arriving in good shape from their direct plane flight to Florida, Barbara told me in a note, Duchess and Duke had a little trouble acclimating to their new southern climate. It had been expected though, and they both soon began to learn about tough Florida grass, air conditioning versus the heat of outdoors, and the benefits of sunscreen. Being mostly black, Duke wasn't much bothered by the southern sun. His skin tolerated it very well. Duchess, however, had to be tended to more carefully. Her white collar, face and little white nose would sunburn easily if sunscreen was not applied diligently. Barb even put a scarf around her neck sometimes to protect her when she was wandering about investigating outdoors. They had a shade tent and kiddy pool in their half of the yard, and the first few weeks of the transition went fairly well.

"They were truly a team," Barb recanted. "Duchess was the dominant one, even though Duke was larger than her, something that would remain true throughout her life. She was always a very serious pig, too. She never met a 'stranger' and would let anyone pet her. There was an air about Duchess that captured the hearts of many, even those who did not meet her in person."

I had the privilege to know Duchess in a way most others didn't. If and when a problem arose, Barb would call to see what I could pick up on and how the pigs felt about things. Usually it was typical herd issues, like Lord chasing the piglets when the opportunity arose. Yet not long after the piglets arrived, Barb and Bob realized that Duchess was deaf. Whether she had been so from birth, or something had taken place after, no one knew for sure. But Duchess still communicated with me, and

Duke became her ears to the world around her. I noticed too that she hummed a lot, as if in a happy little world of her own. No one suspected that something more serious was brewing inside.

Less than a year later, Duchess began to have intermittent seizures. Despite the latest medical technology and drugs, no precedent had been set from previous cases from which to draw some understanding or hope of treating her successfully.

"Duke would stay right by her side, as if to protect and support her when she was sick. Neither Lord nor Lady ever picked on her when she was ill, either," Barb said, with a sorrow in her voice. And with all of the trips to the vet's office or the labs, through all of the tests that she went through for months as they tried to diagnose, then help her, Duchess maintained her wonderful 'air' while letting people poke and prod in an effort to get her well.

Barb and Bob were fortunate to have the best facility to work with right near their home, and Barb stayed, holding Duchess through all of her trips there. No money was spared, nor any suspicion left unexplored, but despite all these efforts Duchess succumbed to liver disease in May 1999. She was barely two years old.

About a week later, while sitting at my desk working, I slowly began to realize I was humming, and as soon as that realization became full in my awareness, Duchess began to speak.

> "I was not a pig of leisure, but rather a pig of great importance. It did not appear to be so when I was born, and my mother did not tell me I had a special job to do, but the Great Pig who looks over us all must have thought I'd be good for the job.
>
> "When I was born it was a special life I lived. With my mother and littermate, I was a happy piglet. When the time came for me to move to my own home, I traveled with my brother and we flew far away. It was a different kind of home we had. It was very warm, it smelled very strange, but there were big pigs, so I knew it must be okay. It surely was.

"I had a people family there ∼ a different kind of herd. Momma and Dad were the biggest people of all, but Army (Armand, her human brother) was big on the inside. I liked to look at him, from time to time, but my favorite place to be was near Momma. It was she who named me Duchess, and Duke became my brother's name. It was said to be a royal herd, because we lived with a Lady and a Lord, too. Lord was one of my favorite pigs, because he liked me so much he'd chase me whenever he could.

"We had a Caroline (her human sister who no longer lived at home), too, but not all the time. Sometimes I would see her, and sometimes I would not. But Caroline always looked at me in a soft way. She must have thought I was beautiful. Of course, I still am.

"I lived a long time with my people family, but I was not meant to live a really long time there. I was meant to be more special. I was meant to be remembered.

"When I was little, I stopped hearing Momma speak my name. Oh, I always heard her call me, but I did not hear with my ears. They stopped working back when I was young.

"When I was older, other things started to go wrong inside, too. But, I did not know what it was all about, and I did not want to ponder it very much. Instead I would hum my days away, doing my chores and getting chased by my friend, Lord.

"Time then came when I would get silly and tip over. These were most distressing to Momma, and I did not like the silly part too much, but it didn't hurt me, so I just tried to forget. For my people, this became a very sad affair, and soon Momma started taking me to many different places where they looked inside to see what was wrong with me. It was then that I really knew I was special, and now I knew what my big job was all about.

"Each day was special with Momma and my herd. I

got special treatment and food stuff because of my insides, but I would tell Lord it was because I was so pretty. It would always make that pig chase me even more. I know that Lord misses chasing me now.

"I don't know when it was, exactly, that the Great Pig decided I'd worked long enough, but one day I got very sick and Momma took me to the clean place. She was all wet on me, and Dad was wet, too. And I was afraid, it's true, because I wasn't sure what was going to happen. One thing was for sure, I was ready to be done working, and later that same day, I came back home ⁓ once through my old herds ⁓ and then to where I am now. Many people call this place heaven, but I will tell you that I call this place my Home.

"I do not remember trotting out of my Duchess bristles, but I do remember nuzzling my brother Duke, whispering into my Lady's ears, and telling my Lord that I'm more beautiful than ever before.

"I do not remember flying far away to my first herd, with mother, but I do remember standing in the yard that I wandered in as a tiny piglet. As I grazed and listened to the whisperings of my first herd, the Great Pig came and told me I was now a whisper unto them! This was not something I expected. It has made me feel very special, important, like a wise one for all pigkind.

"And now, my important work is official. I am remembered with importance to Momma and her people, and I am on the winds of my herd's Knowing, for all of their time, in the world I once lived. Although my bristles are just a part of my memorial, Duchess of Pork has made her special mark upon that world.

"I would like my Momma and my herds to know that I will never stray far. Although they can not see me, I will be more than etched in their hearts ⁓ I will be the shadow on their laps, the warm spot in their bed, the reason Lord looks sideways before spinning out, and the remembrance of a spe-

*cial time … the time when I was given a job by the Great Pig,
and I did it very well.*

   *"So do not cry for me when you think of me gone. I
live on in the hearts of many, and in the important work I did.*

   *"Thank you for letting me be this kind of pig. Thank
you for my life in that world.*

   Duchess"

All who knew Duchess grieved her loss, and Duke missed her most
of all. Her body was privately cremated, a tree planted in her honour,
and some of her ashes were sent back to her original herd in Pennsylvania, to be spread by the winds over the estate on which she was born.
Susan is waiting for Barbara to visit, so that they can do this together.
There is no doubt in my mind that when the time comes Duchess will be
nearby, and as Susan raises the small container to the wind, I know
Lulabelle will be by her side.

In the beginning of the Year 2000, within the domain of
"duchessfund.org" on the World Wide Web, The Duchess Fund™ went
on-line. This charitable, non-profit corporation has created a medical
database, accessible worldwide, to give pet pig owners and veterinary
caregivers access to health-care literature available for potbelly pigs. The
goal is to drastically reduce the number of pet pigs who die before their
time.

   Searchable by symptom or disease name, and based on clinical
cases worldwide, this precious and hard-to-come-by information will
help guide veterinarians into the new world of advanced care for companion pigs. Existing data currently held by individuals, practitioners
and many veterinary universities within the United States is being col-
lected and incorporated into this central database, and more is actively
being sought. Behind this huge and ongoing task is Barbara. Her efforts
to create this wonderful and much-needed database are as tireless as her
love for Duchess and as timeless as her love for all pigs. With this, they
both have truly given a valuable gift to the world, accessible information
that will help pet pigs live longer, healthier lives.

"Duchess' life on this Earth was far too short for me, but now I realize what her goal surely was ∽ the Duchess Fund. Within it, we are all here to continue to love her, forever."

I agree. The health records of all of my pet pigs reside on-line now, along with the surgical records of my good friend, Chrissy Pig, who almost crossed over because of the lack of reliable medical information regarding potbelly pigs at that time.

Anyone who has ever loved a pig can tell you that there's something truly special about this species, something that gets under your skin and changes you in a way you can't even describe. Being able to help them when they fall ill will be easier for vets to do now, thanks to the Duchess Fund. I know that I can think of no memorial more fitting for the sweet little black-and-white, pinto potbelly pig named Duchess of Pork.

And, while keeping in mind how life always go on, Princess Grace arrived in Florida, on a direct flight from Philadelphia, later that same year. She's giving them all a run for their money, while trying to help fill the huge hole that Duchess' crossing left in their lives. Although Duke sometimes still cries for his sister, especially at night, I've no doubt Gracie will be far more than a BandAid for their broken hearts. She is just what this family needed, and I'm thrilled to have known her since piglethood, too. ∽

Aba and Phoebe

"Why don't you ask him a question to start with?" I asked
Cindy, as I tried to form a link with Aba. From past experiences I'd
found this would sometimes get the conversation going, although I
found it very unusual for a horse to need such prodding.

A shooting star streaked through the sky as Cindy and her family stood by the roadside where her horse's body lay. It was a beautiful autumn's night, near midnight, and although she'd have preferred this be just a horrid dream from which she would soon awaken, the truth was she'd been summoned to this spot to deal with her own living nightmare.

Cindy surmised, from the looks of the scene which lay before her, that Aba's death had been instantaneous. Holding back tears, she fell to the ground, and with trembling hands she stroked his lifeless neck.

"How could this have happened?" she asked her husband in disbelief. "Aba *never* tested the fence lines."

Her cousin, Tammy, stood silently in the field, a few yards away, where Aba had been. By her feet lay the body of Phoebe, her pony.

Under the starlit sky they all stood, wrapped in both sorrow and disbelief. The quiet of the night offering up only sounds of their soft sobbing and sniffling. They waited, in near silence, for the neighbors' bulldozer to arrive. Then they would bury their cherished friends.

Cindy called a few days later, asking me to speak with her horse. I was intrigued by the request, and totally unaware of the events that had transpired. I'd known Cindy for a year or so, but never once she had asked me to communicate with any of her animals, even when others around us at a social gathering would ask little questions here and there about their companions at home. I'd been told by an acquaintance that she was a disbeliever in animal communication. So I was pleased that she was now willing to try.

Providing me only with her horses' name, Cindy made an appointment with me for the next afternoon, before her husband would return from work and her young son from school. I assumed she wanted no witnesses to her self-indulgence into what many consider the *unnatural* world of animal communication. I understood. It seems to me that many people in the world simply don't believe that animals are capable of clear and conscious thought. I was anxious to see how Cindy reacted to what her horse would share with her.

Preparing myself the next day for the conversation that was about to begin, I was confused as to why I could not seem to pick up on Aba. In my experience, horses always have something to say, and usually it is of jaw-dropping magnitude. I decided it was probably because she hadn't called in yet, so I waited for her to call.

"I see a brown-and-black horse," I told her when we first started our conversation. I knew this didn't really fit because when we said hello, I asked what colour Aba was, in an effort to form that link I usually have before the phone rings. She told me he was a chestnut-coloured horse.

"Okay, I think I see him. I see white feet," I said, as a very faint picture began to form in mind.

Cindy confirmed that Aba did indeed have two white feet. Confident that I was looking at the correct horse, I began to explain to her that I didn't understand why I was having such trouble picking up on him. There wasn't much else forming in the way of pictures. Aba was not giving me any thought patterns, either, and no distinct feelings were coming through either.

"Why don't you ask him a question," I said.

In the background, I could hear that Cindy was not alone, which surprised me after she'd wanted to book her appointment at a time when her family would be away.

She repeated my request to her audience. The mumbled voices in the background led me to believe there were two other women present, but I could not make out what they were saying. Smiling to myself, I was glad Cindy was sharing this experience with someone else.

"Ask him what happened last Thursday," Cindy finally said. "Ask him how he got hurt."

Instantly I felt a cut, then a cutting pain rip across my chest. Adrenalin rushed through me, and I began to see as if through a horses' eyes. Then just as quickly as these sensations had emerged, time was turned back to those few seconds before the pain had begun. With my heart still in my throat, Aba showed me what had happened just beforehand.

It was very dark outside, and Aba was enjoying a leisurely, quiet, nighttime graze. But the serenity of the moment changed in a split second, when from the corner of my eye I saw a small dog, like a red fox or a young coyote, dart out of the tall grass that grew by the edge of the field. It came straight at my legs, which I now felt I had four of, and as the dog rushed toward me, I suddenly heard the loud report of a gunshot or very large firecracker.

In the next second I saw a boy step out from the woods, behind where the tall grass grew beside the field. Instantly, I felt the horse's body sit back and spin to the right, at the same time pulling a muscle in his back right hip, as he began to plow through a wire fence, which must have only been a few feet away.

"Along with the cutting pain in his chest, his back right leg hurts, too." I said, though barely able to verbalize what I was experiencing as it was happening in a heartbeat's time.

"Did he have a cut on his chest?" I asked Cindy, realizing that he must have torn through a wire fence. "I'm sure Aba didn't realize how close he was to that fence. Going through it was only a mistake made in panic," I said. "I can feel him falling down. Did he scrape his front knees, too?"

As I felt Aba shoot out through the fence in a dead gallop, my vision ended in darkness. Still not understanding the full impact of what I had just been shown, I was confident that this was all that hurt Aba. He shared nothing more than the feelings of panic, the cutting across his chest, a sore back right leg, and scraped-up knees.

"No, he wasn't cut," Cindy's said as her voice trailed off quietly. She put her cousin Tammy on the phone to speak now.

"He was hit by a car last week," Tammy said. "Aba didn't make it."

While I was shocked by this news, it at least made sense to me now ∼ the lack of responding and having been shown what had happened through his own eyes. Aba was "resting" now, on the other side, and just knowing that he had crossed over helped me to understand why the communication proceeded this way.

It is often my experience to find an animal resting, or in a deep sleep, when they have died suddenly and traumatically. I have found this true also, after they have suffered a long, debilitating illness. They tend to rest, it seems, or to fall into a deep, peaceful, healing sleep. Each one varies as to how long that rest will be, too. Even in death, I have found, we retain our individuality as unique beings.

Tammy went on to explain to me that Aba had indeed torn through a wire fence, and ran out into the road that night. Phoebe, her pony, had followed him. They were struck down by the same car that night.

The cut surely must have been there, on Aba's chest, but in their grief, no one examined him closely because there was no hope of saving him. It seemed he had died instantly.

Her leg broken, Phoebe awaited the vet's arrival. Despite her valiant efforts to return to her barn, she was unable to get far and the vet attended to her in the field by the road, not far from her big friend's body.

Unable to be saved, Phoebe, with human loved ones all around her, was euthanized and soon joined Aba in the "Forever Green."

"We didn't know what could have caused them to tear through the fence," Tammy said, in a voice choked with emotion. "Now it makes more sense. We had heard shots in the woods and fields a few days before. We'd heard there were some boys out hunting.

"Does Phoebe say anything to you, Colleen?" she asked, as I could feel her awaiting my response with her breath held.

"Well, she isn't talking, Tammy," I began. "But she is showing me pictures. I'm not sure what they mean.

"She shows me a long, light-coloured mane and tail, which I believe are her own, and the setting is within a beautiful field. Aba is by her side. It is daytime, the sun is shining bright in the sky, and there are butterflies flitting around through the wildflowers that dot the field.

"She also shows me a big rock, one you can sit on to think," I said. "It's a very peaceful, reflective place, Tammy. It's beautiful."

"Oh, I know just what you're talking about," she said confidently. "That's the field where we buried them, together. It does have a big rock nearby, and we've sat there, thinking about them and missing them so much."

Tammy began to tell me about the wildflowers that grow in that pasture, where they'd been that night. And knowing now how much Phoebe seemed to like them, they would plant many more upon the horses' graves.

"I can't begin to tell you how horrible this was for us all," Tammy said in closing. "It was the worst thing we could have ever imagined. But knowing that they are alright, and together, will maybe help us get past this. I don't know. Life is so different without them."

Tammy said good-bye for all who had gathered for this consult, and my heart ached for them, knowing how sad they all were. I thought about how it is one thing to grieve over the loss of a beloved animal, but how much harder it must be when their demise had been so traumatic and unforeseen.

Not long after, a mutual friend told me how much comfort the communication with Aba and Phoebe had brought to Cindy. A new pony now resided in their barn, one which her son would soon begin to ride.

I was glad to hear this news, but felt a little bad at the same time. What a sad way to first experience animal communication, I thought to myself. I wished sadness hadn't been her motivation. ✦

Nike

"She's not saying anything, Aynnie," I told her.
"I don't think she knows what has happened."

Both and indoor and an outdoor cat, Nike very much enjoyed going into the woods behind her house. There appeared to be a place where the neighborhood cats would meet, and she loved to keep her eye on the happenings there. For her human mom, Aynnie, this was good, it was a safe place, away from the busy street at the end of the cul-de-sac where they lived. However, one morning I received a phone call from a tearful Aynnie. Nike had just been hit by a car.

I quickly settled in to communicate with Nike and almost immediately could see her walking toward her house from the street, entering the front yard. She stopped and just stood there, looking at the house. She seemed confused. Although she could see her house, and knew that she was home, somehow things didn't seem quite right. As I began to interpret the feelings Nike was sharing with me, it all became clear ∼ Nike did not realize she had just crossed over.

Being more of an onlooker at this point, I was interested that Nike didn't go in the house. Instead, she sat down on the lawn, staring. I began to speak to her, explaining that she had gone into the busy road and been hit by a car. And, as I spoke, I became aware of an older woman approaching Nike from behind.

She wore a long dress with an apron on top, both amply covered her stout frame. Her hair was white, pulled back into a loosely knotted bun. Her beautiful, loving eyes captivated me most ∼ they looked like sun-dappled blue water. After being lost in the scene before me for a moment or two, I noticed she carried a box with her. And, as I watched her walk toward Nike, I had the distinct feeling that this woman did not even notice me. She was there for Nike alone.

Slowly, the old woman approached Nike, stopping to stand by her side. Lovingly, she looked down at the confused little cat. Nike looked up. Then, ever so gently, the old woman reached down and patted Nike on the head, at the same time setting the box on the ground beside them both.

Nike stood back up, looked at the box, then returned her focus to the house. For a minute or so they both stood there silently, the old woman bent over, stroking Nike's head, while Nike looked at her old home.

I could sense that the old woman was speaking to Nike, but I couldn't make out what she was saying. The words were not for me ∼ but the feeling was that of utter love.

Finally the old woman reached over and fluffed a blanket that had been lying in the bottom of the box. Picking up Nike, she gently placed her inside it, upon the blanket, then carefully lifted them both.

She turned, walked away, and the vision quickly faded. Now it was quite clear to me that this woman would care for Nike in her first moments on the other side of life. And, as I conveyed all of this to Aynnie, who sat listening quietly on the other end of the phone, I could here her sniffle, through a sigh of relief.

Aynnie told me she felt better about where Nike was, and she knew Nike was going to be okay. Assuring her that I believed that too, we said our good-byes and ended our communication.

The rest of the day I was left with the most beautiful feelings inside. Feelings of tenderness and love, kindness and sharing, and the indescribable soothing I'd felt when I looked into the old woman's beautiful blue eyes.

It was a comfort to know that Nike was not alone, and that someone was there to help her understand what had just happened and where she now was. And although this was only the first time I'd seen the old woman, and the box into which she put recently departed cats, it wasn't long before I found that it would not be the last.

All in all, I believe I've seen the old woman come to the aid of five more bewildered cats, and with the last one, Nike came with her. ❧

Kismet

Speaking quietly and telepathically, respectful of the moment at hand, I began to relay the information to Kismet that her mom, Aynnie, wished her to know. It had been a few years since their friend Nike had crossed over to the Rainbow Bridge, and now it was Kismet's turn.

"Don't be afraid, Kismet," I said.
"The vet is coming in just a few minutes now, then everyone with you will help you cross over to the Rainbow Bridge."

An old cat who recently began suffering from some form of skin disease that baffled her vets, Kismet struggled until the very end to hold onto a body that could no longer support her physical life.

I had spoken to Kismet and her family just the week before. She had told us then that she was not yet ready to go. She explained how she really loved her family, and her other kitty friends in their home, and she was not ready to leave them behind.

Her diseased state, however, did not offer options to try that could possibly help her keep going. Nothing could be done, and it was felt that the skin lesions and lumps all over her body were only the tip of a deeper problem going on inside.

Her days since our last talk were spent at home, family by her side, hearing encouraging messages of how it was okay to go. She lingered though, complaining of a terrible headache, while attending to her family as best she could. Believing Kismet was nearing her final moments in this world, and unable to bear seeing her suffer any longer, Aynnie finally made two emotionally difficult calls: one to arrange for her euthanasia, and the other to me, to make arrangements for her spiritual departure.

Moments before the vet was to arrive, I told Kismet not to be afraid, that she would soon be free of her old, worn-out body. I noticed how Kismet seemed to feel out-of-sorts, and she willingly showed me the spots on her body, noting how now they were all black inside, too. Kismet went on to say that she felt they had taken her over, and she simply could not fight them anymore. As the doorbell rang, I conveyed Kismet's message to Aynnie, then I hung up the phone feeling confident that Kismet was now truly ready to move on.

Sitting at my desk I pictured Kismet in my mind, imagining how she felt as she left her physical body and journeyed to the other side. I showed her what other animals had shown me when they had crossed over, then I lovingly bid her farewell, and a speedy journey.

Aynnie told me, soon after it was done, that thanks to the gentle vet who made the house call that morning, Kismet had crossed over both quickly and quietly, in her own home, with her human mom at her side.

Later that same day my thoughts were brought back to Kismet, when I suddenly saw her sitting before me, smiling.

"What an ordeal!" she said in a voice that was undeniably strong as she referred to her illness. "I'm glad that's over."

I looked at how beautiful the cat before me now was. She radiated with health and vitality, and with no apparent lumps or lesions from the disease from which she had suffered just hours before.

"I'm so happy to see you, Kismet! That was fast!" I exclaimed, briefly startled by her sudden appearance. "Look at you ∼ you are your old, beautiful self ∼ with no lumps!"

The cat beamed at me, then quietly sat down so that I could get a good look at her. I marveled at the radiance she now emitted, and then noticed she was sitting in a box, with her old pal, Nike, sitting beside her. Looking over their shoulders, I sighed a deep sigh of recognition as I saw the same old woman who had first helped Nike in her hour of need. She was there, standing off in the distance, and it seemed like I sat there a long time, in this new world, looking at these three.

Love and joy filled my whole chest like a deep, full breath of a summer morning's dew-filled air. Then, just before the scene started to fade from view, Kismet conveyed to me that she'd crossed over in a full waking state.

"I saw many sparkles and then I knew I didn't have to have that headache anymore," she whispered, then she vanished, although the joy remained for me to savor for some time.

Slowly becoming aware of my surroundings again, I reached for a notepad and pen, writing down for her family the wonderful experience I had just been privileged to enjoy.

"Although she is now gone, she didn't convey to me any plans for moving on yet in the other worlds," I wrote. Finishing my note, I addressed an envelope, put on a stamp, then went to find my shoes.

Walking to the mailbox I reflected back over the day's events, and how Kismet had worried about leaving her family behind. My heart filled with elation while my eyes filled with joyful tears. I reflected on how Kismet had found something just as beautiful in heaven as her people had been to her here on Earth.

As I dropped the notecard into the mailbox and pulled the red flag up on the side, I pictured again that last fleeting picture she'd shared. Kismet, just sitting there, in that box with a soft blanket beneath her, and her old friend, Nike, at her side. ⬦

Wild Dog

"People are petting me," he said,
in the only words I ever heard him utter.

Coyotes were creatures I'd only heard sometimes at night as they'd howl under moonlit skies. My first glimpse of one came late one cold winter's afternoon, as the sun began to sink behind the ridge across the water. Facing the river, our picture window lent a perfect frame to the wintry scene outside. On this day, a female dog, different than any other dog I'd ever seen before, sat quietly, crouched near the edge of the ice. In the hush of the ending day, she watched ducks swim nonchalantly in the water only a few feet away.

"If you jump for a duck, you're going to get very cold, very fast," I said to her without thinking, but the wild dog did not seem to hear me. Slowly, she reached out one foot and half-heartedly slapped at the frigid water before her. The ducks merely flapped a few wings and quacked a few quacks. Then the whole flock swam a little further out into open water.

Winter, so far that year, had been hard on the local wildlife. We'd heard reports of warnings issued to suburbanites to be on the look out for coyotes coming in close to homes in search of food. Protecting their livestock, farmers were shooting them on sight, and we'd heard stories of how vicious a pack of coy-dogs could be.

On Wild Dog, I could easily see the truth of the hardships this winter was giving her. As she rose to walk away from the water's edge, I could see her skin hanging beneath her, as if she'd not eaten in a long time. The ducks we'd been feeding were as plump as ever, though. One surely would have been a welcome meal for Wild Dog, had she found good fortune hunting that day.

I watched her slowly walk down the edge of the ice as I imagined what her life must be like, especially now that humans were on the look-out for her kind. Had the snow not been so deep, and the temperatures not remained near zero for three weeks in a row, perhaps she wouldn't have found herself so close to humans, as she searched for a life-saving meal.

She squatted to relieve her bladder before heading toward the ridge, and I *almost* wished I could toss her some food to eat. But, the river was too wide, and I knew an act of kindness like this would surely jeopardize her life. I simply couldn't draw her near to our home for a meal. Not to where our pet pigs grazed in good weather.

As she disappeared into the woods, I turned to walk away. Although the snow prevented them from going anywhere near the river now, it was time for our pigs to get off the sofas and head outdoors for a warm winter meal.

They complained and fussed as I hurried them onward to their awaiting polar fleece winter capes. While buckling them around each pig's neck and potbelly, I let my thoughts began to drift away from the plight of the wild animals that winter. But, in the last fleeting moment that I thought about Wild Dog and how hungry she must have been, I was thankful that these pampered porcine would never know that kind of existence.

Opening the door, they barreled outside onto the freshly shoveled walkway and dove into their bowls of warmed, wet feed that I make especially for them. I then grabbed a shovel and proceeded to clear a place for them to potty that would be out of the wind, which had suddenly begun to blow.

It was late afternoon and high winds blew snow off the tops of all snowbanks that lined the edge of the road as Wayne and I were returning home from the store. With the sun setting and the wind driving snow horizontally across the road, visibility was very poor. As we approached the back entrance of the new mall, which had been built a few years before upon acres of previously wooded farm land, I noticed three people huddled on the side of the road.

"Do you see those people there, Wayne?" I asked.

Lost temporarily in the white-out, and barely visible on the shoulder of the road between us and the huddled mass, was a white truck. As my foot reached for the imaginary brake on the passenger's side of the car, Wayne took his foot off the accelerator and the car began to slow.

"Yes, I see it," he calmly said, glimpsing over to my foot that was pressing to the floorboard as if it would help slow us down at all.

I had been nervous beforehand because it was hard to see, but the white sheet lying over the dog on the ground wasn't. As we slowly passed by, one person bent down to reposition the sheet before adding a blanket on top. She lifted it up just as we passed by, and I could plainly see it was a coyote, just like Wild Dog, and it lay there helpless and hurt on the side of the cold, snowy road.

"Oh, where is it?" I half-shouted as I grabbed for my purse, frantically searching for Arnica, the homeopathic first-aid remedy used for traumas such as this. Our car had come to a stop as I realized the Arnica was not to be found, and turning around to peer out the back window, Wayne began backing the car up toward the accident scene before I even had the chance to ask.

"Can we help you any here?" he asked the man, who was closest to our car. "We can put the dog in the car and take it to our vet. He's just down the road two miles on the left."

"No, but thanks anyway," the fellow said as he hugged himself trying to create a little extra warmth against the bitter cold winds. He looked back toward two women, who were now draping the folded blanket over the sheet on the ground.

"It's not our dog," he said sadly. "We don't know whose he is because he doesn't have a collar on. He's bleeding heavily from his mouth, too. It doesn't look good."

"He just came running out of the driveway over there and I couldn't stop or avoid him," he said, the despair in his voice very evident. And, as he reached up with one hand to pull his collar up further around his neck, his other hand tightly gripped a cell phone. "The police are on the way," he mumbled.

I looked toward where he had pointed and could see animal tracks in the fresh, wind swept snow. They came from the open field behind the house and down the driveway, where they ended at the street's edge. As Wayne began to pull our car away before traffic piled up behind us, I thought to myself that these people must not realize that it was a coyote they had struck with their truck. This was not somebody's pet.

"He must have been coming in closer to look for food," I said as the car picked up a little speed and the scene out of the back window began to grow smaller.

I wanted to stay, but I knew there was nothing I could physically do to help. In a moment of clarity I realized that I could do something indeed ∼ I could talk to this apparent coy-dog who lay there hurt, because telepathy knows no distance boundaries.

As the car moved slowly along the slick road before us, I closed my eyes for only a second before I saw myself standing near the coy-dog. He stood quietly by my side watching his physical self lay in the road. He was taking special note of the two women standing close to his body, then he glanced over to the man who still stood in the road, his cell phone in hand ready to dial for help again.

The coy-dog seemed to be out of his body one second and in it the next. It seemed he wasn't going to make it because it felt like he was at breath's end.

"It's okay to go if you need to," I told him, but the only response he gave to me was by sharing some pictures from his life and a few thoughts regarding the moment at hand. He was focusing on the people with him and for a good reason.

The pictures were of being a wild dog, and he did look the part from what I saw when we passed. And he was stunned that people were now with him.

"People are petting me," he said, in the only words I ever heard him utter. As he spoke them I could feel soft, gentle hands lightly stroking his head between his upright ears. It seemed that this coy-dog hadn't felt this kind of softness since he was a pup, and in that moment I believed it was something he'd take with him when he left.

Quickly as it had begun, the communication tie was severed and I found our car pulling onto our road, only a few doors from home.

"It's strange how this has affected me," I told my husband as we opened the car doors and braced ourselves against the strong wind. "I can't believe I didn't insist on getting out to try and help," I said. Yet, as I heard myself saying these words, somewhere inside me I knew that I didn't really belong there.

Had we picked him up and taken him to our vet as offered, I don't think his ending would have been as fulfilling. The beautiful feelings I felt from him as he watched and experienced people loving him, in his last minutes of life after being struck down, were like a gift of insight that touched his very soul. And from what I had seen, it touched the hearts of the three people who stayed with him until the end.

A month later I saw Wild Dog once again on the ice, and this time a friend followed her. She still half-heartedly approaching the ducks that slept on the frozen river's edge, yet no wings flapped or quacks sounded, as the ducks found these two intruders no threat to their peaceful afternoon nap.

In amazement, I watched Wild Dog approach within a few feet of the ducks, before she casually turned away and walked slowly on down the ice, her friend trailing behind her in the same casual manner. Had they been hungry, they surely would have tried for the sleeping ducks.

Winter was beginning to fade, and as the sun shone high and warm in the sky, the record breaking snowfall began to slowly melt, and my heart was warmed by the thought that the ground cover had not kept these two from enjoying a good meal. Starvation wouldn't be their fate this winter if they could hold out just a short time longer.

Before long, the song birds would be returning, flowers blooming and food plentiful again for the wild animals, too. And as Wild Dog and her friend disappeared into the woods across the river, I too walked away, with a new respect for all life, and for the beauty one can find in even some of life's sad moments. ❧

Tiffany

"I'd like to have a talk with Tiffany, Colleen.
When can you fit us in?"

After a hectic month at school, MaryLea had just finished taking her college finals, giving her time for some much needed relaxation and catching up. It was just two weeks before Christmas, and she wanted to start her holiday vacation by touching base with her cat.

A beautiful, male cat, Tiffany was very pleasant and light-hearted. As he spoke, it became clear that he loved the Christmas season, and even made a short Christmas list of his own ∼ a few little things that he hoped he would get.

Tiffany told how much he loved the holiday lights that lit their tree each year. His favorite were the candles in the windows that beckoned one in on a cold winter's night.

"Where is my kitchen window candle?" he asked. "The one I can see from my backyard?"

MaryLea apologized for not having tended to the decorations yet this year. She had been so tired getting home from work and school that she had simply put it off.

"This weekend we will decorate, Tiffany," she assured him. "I'll do your candle first."

Then he asked for a small toy, the first time an animal had offered up a Christmas wish list to me. As I chuckled to myself, MaryLea promised that it would all be done right away and his wish list would not be forgotten. Our conversation happily ended and I went on to work on my own family's wish lists.

The very next day, early in the evening, I received a frantic call. MaryLea had just returned home to find Tiffany lying lifeless on the kitchen floor. Because of her sudden shock and sorrow, I had trouble concentrating on Tiffany and tried instead to soothe her broken heart.

"I don't know what happened, Colleen!" she said. "I just walked in, and he didn't come as usual. I found him here in the kitchen and I don't know what to do. I was shopping, and I bought him a present." Her voice trailed off, and I tried to concentrate.

I could feel Tiffany there as strongly as I had the night before. He was not frightened, but rather confused. As I spoke with him, wondering what had happened, the first and repeating message that I kept getting was how this was not planned, it was an accident. I kept seeing a very small, black, round thing and I felt a lump in my throat. I believed he had choked on something.

After explaining what Tiffany shared with me, MaryLea and I ended our conversation with the promise of a return call in the morning. She needed to go and lay her beloved friend to rest, and I wanted to sit quietly to give Tiffany my full attention.

My session with Tiffany revealed many things to me about the process of "sudden death." I asked Tiffany to show me what had happened to him. He did. Through his pictures I could see that it had been getting dark outside when he went into the kitchen, awaiting his mom's return. He started gagging, then all of a sudden he was in a different place.

He showed me himself in a very misty place, devoid of any discernible surroundings except for a view of his kitchen, where he'd just been. He was confused about what had happened so quickly to him. Seeing his body lying on the floor, Tiffany began to realize that he had crossed over.

"Why?" he asked me, but I did not know what to tell him.

He told me that he became very worried about his mom coming home and finding him like that. He knew she would be sad, but he also was very embarrassed at how he looked lying there on the floor. He remained very concerned about this until she walked in the door and found him. He began to realize what this all meant and many revelations began to open up to him ∽ he had choked to death. This was not in his plans.

Tiffany said he hadn't realized it was time for him to cross over, and he was a bit sad because he would have planned it better. It was okay that he was here. He did not hurt and he was not afraid. But he did not like having his mom see him like that. Had he known it was time to go, he would have done it outdoors, he told me.

I took the time to write down everything that Tiffany had to say. When MaryLea phoned the next morning, I read it to her as I pictured him sitting on the arm of their favorite chair, the one in which she now sat alone. When I was done, she confided that she did indeed believe he had choked.

"I always left three vitamin pills in his breakfast dish each day," she said, sobbing and trying to catch her breath. "This morning when I went to pick up his dish to clean it, there were two pills there. One small, dark, round vitamin pill was missing."

My heart ached for MaryLea, and I wondered if her grief was causing her to feel responsible for Tiffany's death. I didn't think she should feel that way at all, but it seems we are usually our own worst critic, especially when the loss of a loved one is involved.

MaryLea asked me to convey to Tiffany how much she loved him. His response was a gift in itself.

"Here, love is as abundant as the worlds are many, as the universe is wide. This is a nice place to be," Tiffany said without hesitation.

MaryLea repeated his words back, out loud, and after a moment or two of silence, I could hear her sigh deeply. For now the tears had subsided, and MaryLea lingered within the majestic picture her cat had just painted with words. But I was already disheartened, knowing that mere words could never really convey to her all that Tiffany had shared. The pictures and feelings that went along with the words were awe inspiring. For these, there simply were no words.

What a pitiful form of communication language really is, I thought to myself, compared to the illustrious universal language we humans seemed to have let go. Believing her cherished friend was well, even though not physically with her, would help MaryLea through her grief.

Saying good-bye and hanging up my phone, I paused for a moment to wish Tiffany well in his new life. The cat seemed pleased, and the pictures began to fade.

Marylea would miss her friend dearly. She had lots of wonderful memories that she would hold dear in her heart. And no doubt, she would always think of Tiffany whenever she gazed upon a candlelit window. ☙

Spike and Friends ～ Pigs of Great Fortune!

*"We left our bristles at the hands of humans,
and this is what we would like to help you understand ..."*

Even though I believe that death is not the end, cruelty and slaughter have got to be the hardest methods of an animal's crossing over for humans to deal with emotionally. Whether word of it comes to me via a consult or the news, each time I am reassured as to why I prefer to work with animals instead of mankind.

I have no tolerance toward humans who torture animals for any reason, yet I do recognize the depth to which their sickness goes to allow them to commit these heinous acts. The rescue shelters and sanctuaries that I have worked with have shown me a side of life that, like many, I would rather believe not exists. Yet, day after day, animals are rescued from one horrendous situation after the other, and the people who commit these inhumane crimes most often go unpunished. For many rescuers, bearing witness to this injustice leaves a deep wound that never heals and haunts them at every turn.

Pigs, in general, are amazing creatures, and I wish more people knew this. The fourth-smartest species on the planet, pigs fall in line just behind humans, primates, and whales/dolphins. Their lateral-thinking and problem-solving abilities make pigs far more intelligent than your average dog or cat and in my experience, more intelligent than many people I know. The majority of humans have no idea how much so. Pigs are also very social and herd (family) oriented. People who keep pigs as pets will tell you that they are the most intriguing beings with whom they have ever shared their lives. They are capable of the greatest love and devotion and have been known to grieve horrendously when separated from their family, many times with real tears running down their cheeks.

As Vietnamese potbelly pigs came into our country's marketplace, becoming the 1980's exotic new pet-to-have, humans found a new throwaway commodity. Rescue shelters have sprung up across the nation to help these pigs-in-need, thanks to backyard breeders who unscrupulously pumped out crossbred piglets, then sold them to uninformed humans with no understanding of their natural tendencies, needs and probable full-grown size. Greed and ignorance have put the potbelly pig in a devastating situation ∼ much like other species man has supposedly befriended.

It's hard to endure the abuse of any living creature, and for those who can "hear," it is harder still when the voice heard speaks with incredible wisdom. To lose an intelligent being, no matter their species or their size, is always a loss to the world.

In the late spring of 1996, I was called in on a missing pigs case in Florida. A sanctuary that I had begun consulting for the winter before asked me if I could help locate a few missing potbelly pigs from an overflow shelter. They gave me the names of two of the pigs, Spike and Annabelle, then began to briefly tell me when they had turned up missing.

Overwhelming feelings of terror and panic swept over me. I could see some "backwoods" surroundings, but my vision was clouded by the tears streaming down my face and the indescribable panic welling up inside of me. I was caught completely off-guard.

"I don't know how to tell you this, but I think these animals were slaughtered." The words on the audiotape that was recording the communication were broken up with emotion as I tried to catch my breath. Never had I been so overwhelmed!

"We've been afraid that's what happened to them," Becky replied, then she and Linda waited patiently for me to regain some composure before going on. "One of the other women here knows a well-known psychic. She asked him for his help and he told her that he thought they had been slaughtered, too. Can you give us any information that might help us find who did this?"

Not knowing beforehand what they had suspected, I was not prepared at all for what I had just tuned into, undoubtedly making it all much harder to handle. I felt paralyzed with shock. I had never dreamed how terrified one could truly feel. Unable to pay attention to what Becky was saying, I had to end the session in order to clear these feelings away. I told her that I would sit down later to do this consult alone, and then I'd let them know whatever information came through. I waited three days.

Refusing to watch most television newscasts and purposely avoiding the newspaper as much as possible, I shelter myself from a lot of life's cruelties. This experience showed me how crippling emotions can truly be. I had been of no help at that moment as fear, grief, shock and horror grabbed hold of me. Detaching myself from such gripping emotions is the only way that I can truly help those in need. I believed that Spike's and Annabelle's physical demise was either in progress or occurred relatively closely to that time when I was asked to speak with them. There was nothing I could do to help any of them at that moment ∼ but I was anxious to communicate to the pigs my grave sorrow, much of it felt for my own species. When I later sat down to speak with them, I was amazed at their greeting.

Instantly I was enveloped with a light-heartedness that I was now becoming familiar with from other animals shortly after they had crossed over. They surprised me, considering what I had felt just three days before. Five pigs were standing before me as I sat with my eyes closed, and although they communicated as a group, Spikey was the one directly relaying their message. I introduced myself and told them that I was there on behalf of many humans who were concerned for their well-being.

"Many people are worried about you. They are so very sorry that they left you at that shelter, and they desperately tried to find you. They are very sad about what has happened to you all, and they are trying very hard to find the people responsible so that they can be punished for this."

Five smiling pigs looked back at me as unconditional love swept over every inch of my being, soothing my own thoughts of what these pigs had recently gone through. I sat back, put my fingers to my keyboard, and brought to words the blocks of thoughts, feelings and joy they all conveyed. Their message lifted my heart and proved to me, yet again, that when we step from this life to the next, negative emotions are left behind. This place where we now live is but a school, a place to learn, and when we are through, we take our lessons learned and move on to the next new experience.

> "My Dearest Human Friends,
>
> "This is Spikey, and I am here to speak with you, along with my good friends Annabelle, Mike, Chuck and Gretchen. We would like you to listen and take the time to understand what we have to say. We truly enjoy being able to communicate with you on this level ⁓ it is very clean and happy ⁓ just as what it is we would like to share.
>
> "As you remember, all of my friends are here because of man. We have all entered this nonphysical stage of life due to the abrupt ending of our physical bodies, which was no apparent fault of our own. We left our bristles at the hands of humans, which is okay! This is what we would like to help you understand ...
>
> "One thing you should strive to remember, when your heart is crying at the loss of me, or another, is that we are still here speaking to you. There is no death! That very essence of who I am lives on, as it does for all living beings upon our home, our planet, our physical world. It is a wonderful opportunity to be there in a physical body and why is that? Because we have a greater opportunity to learn! Learn what? Lessons that we have chosen to learn before we take our form! This is

a wonderful thing!

"*Each of us is in control of exactly what we would like to accomplish, before deciding just how we would like to do it. This is the wonderfulness of life, whether it be here in the nonphysical light worlds, or there in the dense, heavy physical worlds. We will tell you that the lessons learned there do just seem to have more weight, no joke intended.*

"*All beings strive to have opportunities to benefit from, and we do this many lifetimes over. This is why we are still able to speak with you now. The cycle of physical birth, and birth into the nonphysical, and yet back into the physical again is the true 'Circle of Life.' Often, it is misunderstood by humans, who believe that life and death is the life circle. But we tell you it is not, because there is really no death. There is no ending.*

"*We have spoken about this with each other, and want to help you understand that you need not try to bring justice to those who were responsible for any of our physical endings. It is not important now. We would ask you to focus upon two truths: The first is that we create our own lesson plan unto which we, alone, will decide the experiences put upon it. And the second is that we all learn those lessons, in one lifetime or another.*

"In our travels through time-gates of the living
into the worlds we have chosen to learn,
our minds remember none of the lessons
of benchmarks upon paths which we'd earned.

"For those who kept us from our bristles,
on an earth-world that we had come to,
will carry the lessons deep in their beings
and will relearn them before they are through.

"Those humans who hurt us so deep,
are people just trying to adapt
to the lessons they chose to encounter,
so this was not a senseless mishap.

"You see, we have learned lessons as they have,
which will help us to our great reward,
like the eagle which soars to the heavens
and flies through the clouds evermore.

"We bid you now peace in your dream worlds,
which carry you through life's great gates
to greater viewpoints about lessons
which will bring you true wisdom, not hate.

"No one is less of a great being
than the other who travels different ways.
We all will find wisdom eternally,
And we all will find glory one day.

"The Glory of Life is the knowledge
that peace, love and joy are our right,
to have, and to hold in us daily,
if we keep lessons clear in our sight.

"So, don't be sad or misled in your thinking
that bad things are a terrible wrong.
They're just more steps upon a great journey,
which gives Life its sweetest love song.

"The Blessings of Life are unending
as is the love that comes from a pure heart.
So now go and find joy in your travels
as it is time for us to part.

"We will seek lessons which we wish to join in
that will take us to new places now.
Your cares have given us new direction
to be cow, dog or bird ⏜ maybe sow.

"We may have been pigs in your lifetime
but lessons are unlimited events
to try many paths on our journey onward
and not one will be ever misspent.

"We bid thee farewell for the meantime,
but remember us in your life at times.
You may cross our path in your future,
which will prove that there are no good-byes.

"Your friends,
Spike, Annabelle, Chuck, Mike and Gretchen
Pigs of Great Fortune!"

By no means does this even slightly imply to me that I believe abuse, cruelty or slaughter should ever be deemed acceptable in our society, whether or not one believes life to be never-ending. Rather, it merely means that there may be a reason why, and also a hope of greater compassion to hold onto when faced with the feelings that you weren't able to immediately help a being in need.

Many people read Spike's message before this book was sent to press, and they have relayed to me that its beauty and depth are so far reaching that it has helped them endure the senseless acts some humans thrust upon the animal kingdom. I know that it helps me. This case was exceptionally poignant because the woman in charge of this shelter was responsible for the outcome, and I believe this alone points out something very important to think about, indeed.

People who open their hearts and homes to abandoned, abused, neglected and orphaned animals truly deserve the help, admiration and support of the rest of us. The world is a better place for their commitment and dedication to the animals. It takes a compassionate and strong person to willingly take an animal's broken body and help nurture it back to health. Countless, thankless hours go into their physical recuperation, and *then* the real work often begins ∼ the healing of Soul. For those people I hope that Spike's message will be even more meaningful, because too often they lose those in their charge.

I have worked with many shelters and rescue facilities in the years since receiving Spike's message. One of the hardest things for me to face now is good-hearted people opening their homes to *too many* animals in need. There comes a time when we must realize and accept that there is a limit to our own personal abilities and resources. Taking in more animals than you can properly care for is a cruelty in itself. Food, water and shelter are not enough, neither is just love. Each animal in human care should have available to it the individual medical, nutritional and emotional attention needed, and deserved, *daily*. When this can't be provided, the animals are exchanging one bad situation for another. While they may not be in physical danger anymore, without an emotional quality to life, where is the gift?

This "overflow" shelter in question had no excuse to not provide for these pigs. So what went wrong? Did they just become greedy, or did they burn out? These are questions that will never be answered, and those who sought out her help are still learning to live with their own consciences after entrusting these pigs into that shelter's care. Sadly, some admit their inner voice advised caution, but they convinced themselves the pigs would be alright, because the word "Shelter" was written on the door.

We can't go back and fix the mistakes we have made in life, we can only learn from them and take the new knowledge with us as we travel on to new experiences. Inspired by Spike's story, central Florida now hosts yet another rescue group that networks with a number of pig shelters nationwide. In a state where backyard breeders run rampant and abandoned pigs are left in the woods to fend for themselves (which they can't), this group, like others in Florida, is helping large numbers of throwaway and abused pigs find sanctuary, while making great strides to inform the public about the proper way to care for pet pigs. They have been given my permission to take one line from Spike's message with which to name their new group: Pigs of Great Fortune is open for business, but we all hope it will close one day ∼ for lack of pigs-in-need.

This was the first cruelty case that I had ever experienced. In the years since I have been called in on only a handful more. They aren't much easier to handle in the moment, but as soon as the link is broken or the animal has crossed over, the feelings return to peacefulness and the messages are most inspiring. I rest more comfortably knowing that even the animals believe that life here is chosen for the experience. Yet I also would like to believe that there will be a time in our world when cruelty no longer exists for any species of animal ∼ human included.

The respect born out of the mere *willingness* to listen will, I believe, create a sanctity for life that all beings will enjoy. In this I find comfort, and I thank these five pigs for sharing with me an insight that has changed my life forever. ❧

Sundancer

*"I just took a big jump ⌒ it was like leaping into the mist.
I felt coolness on my face, and the smell was just so clean and
light. I really liked it and I haven't used my claws once."*

"I wonder what he meant by that?" Pam asked.

Still processing everything that had been put before me, I replied, "I think that there was just never an inkling of fear, not even when she came and gave him the injection, because he knew what was coming and he was ready to go."

This was my first conversation with Sundancer and Pam after Sundancer's crossing, and I entered into it with some sadness, having conversed with them before. As I cautiously started sorting it out, he was very careful that the words I formed in my mind were the appropriate ones.

A Maine Coon cat who came to Pam as a young kitten, Sundancer was sickly from the start ... well, the vet said he was, but Sundancer never really admitted to it. Harmony, his housemate of the same breed, was also not well. For some reason, Pam had attracted two cats in need, after losing two older cats she'd had many years.

"He's very happy, and he's very thankful that he didn't have to be embarrassed about his condition when he finally crossed over," I relayed. "This was much nicer for him, he tells me. He has a very light feel about him, very, very ... like bliss. That's the best word I can use. He's just like this big ball of yellow with two eyes. He says that he glows in the dark now."

Before our scheduled appointment, I hadn't needed to sit down as usual to tune into him because Sundancer was instantly there. I asked him if he could please hold on until his mom rang through on the phone, and he smiled at me, while giving me an agreeing feeling. I could tell he had much to say and a true happiness engulfed me.

"He's just so happy in the awareness that he doesn't have breathing problems. All of that stuff is gone," I conveyed when Pam called. Sundancer added, "I'm the happiest of cats."

Like many animal guardians following a euthanasia, Pam expressed concern that Sundancer had not been ready to go, particularly because in this case his body had remained up and moving after his first injection.

Sundancer instantly jumped in to explain his behavior. "He says he's sorry that he ran around on you. It wasn't that he was afraid of you, he just had a lot of energy. He played all day and the night before not because he didn't want to go, but because it was his party. He was thankful that you played with him all that time."

Sundancer showed me that after the vet had given him his first injection, he had experimented, almost like a puppeteer, to see if he could make his body do what he wanted even though he wasn't in it. "It didn't work very well," he commented.

He went on to say that he really liked "that lady," the veterinarian whose in-home transition services enabled him to cross over at home, in his favorite place. He appreciated not having to go to a vet's office ∼ it really meant a lot to him. By offering this option, she gives animals the opportunity to cross over in the familiar, loving surroundings they've lived in, instead of a cold, clinical, strange-smelling office which often strikes terrible fear into the hearts even of animals who only just pull into its parking lot. I had never heard of small-animal veterinarians offering this before, and my mind wandered as I imagined how wonderful it would be if more did. I did not stay in the thought long, as Harmony brought my attention back quickly.

She will be my lady, too," he said. "She talked to me. She said that

I am a very nice cat and she is sorry for my loss."

Harmony went on to describe her as very nice and very warm. No doubt he was referring to her extremely genuine care and concern for their feelings, along with their dignity as sentient beings.

Pam then spoke about how the vet had arrived late because of an emergency, and how it seemed to her that the later it got, the more it felt like Sundancer almost "wasn't there." Oftentimes, I have found, when an animal is very ill or near death, it prefers not to stay in its body. The essence of who they are travels outside the physical shell, but does not go far. Sundancer confirmed that this was just what he was doing.

"I was doing the in-and-out thing," he said. "I was there, sitting with Harmony." I quickly learned that this would have required Sundancer to, indeed, be out-of-body because Harmony was in another room at the time.

Both cats knew that a transition was about to take place that evening, and I felt that Sundancer had worried more about Harmony, his best friend, than anything else. This would be a sad time for his buddy.

Sundancer went on to convey that he hadn't really ventured very far in his new, light state either. He explored his new domain mostly at night, while Pam and Harmony were sleeping, but during the day, Sundancer said, he still snuggled with Harmony for catnaps. "Even though we still sleep together, I'm not warm to him now," Sundancer said, his words coming with acknowledgment from Harmony. At times I wasn't sure whose thoughts I was receiving, as both cats showed me pictures of still being together.

Sundancer said that Harmony missed him, but that his friend was getting along okay and was looking forward to not missing him much longer. Harmony's plan now was to enjoy the time that it would be just him and Mom. From this I gathered that Sundancer apparently felt that his need to stay close was really more for Harmony than Pam, and that already it was becoming less needful. He felt that Pam was okay with his crossing over. After all, they always believed that she would be speaking with him again.

"Will you tell us what you've already found?" Pam asked.

Quickly, Sundancer showed me a picture of the nicest little hole in the ground. "It's big enough for a cat to get inside," he said. "And when you go down into the hole, there's a whole family of mice there. I only sniff them though and look them over, but I don't do anything else."

The picture I was seeing was so sweet. It reminded me of a children's picture book.

"I guess it's Mouse Heaven," he said, and we both began to laugh.

"I like it when you sing to me, and maybe you could sing more? That's how I got my name." Harmony had turned our attention to him again, and Pam confirmed that she did like to sing about the house and often made up songs with the cats names in them.

"They seem to like that a lot," she told me.

"I hear music a lot, but it's not music like … " I paused to decipher what Harmony was giving next; it was a picture. "… it's more like tinkling sounds, as if in a breeze. He likes it a lot and he's showing me a lot more yellow. It's as if the sky is all yellow but I don't know if I am looking at a sky or if I'm looking at him as a big ball of yellow."

Neither Pam nor I were sure what this meant, so Pam went on to inquire whether Harmony was alright. She had once asked him in a previous consult about whether he would like another companion so that he wouldn't be lonely without Sundancer one day. His thoughts on this were still the same.

"If you get another cat it would not make me feel happier because it's not Sundancer." He went on to explain that he felt too old to deal with another cat, so he didn't want to. "It would wear me out," he said. "I don't want to wear out that fast."

We could understand. Harmony had health problems of his own and he had never enjoyed being the only cat before. He was very much looking forward to it now. It was a time for both of them to heal their emotional wounds and form a new, stronger bond of their own, together. Pam understood completely. Harmony wanted to help himself begin this process, and asked if he could to talk more about Sundancer's crossing.

"I saw him go! He took a big jump up, straight up in the air, and it was really nice. He was all sparkles, so I am calling him Twinkle Toes now." As giggles filled the phone lines, Harmony showed me a picture of what he saw. It looked like a big sunburst from fireworks, the kind that looks like a great big ball with tons of sparkles in it.

We all paused a moment to relish the picture in our mind and I'm sure that smiles were on the faces of all involved, and not just mine. I felt the exhilaration I get when at a Fourth of July celebration. What a magnificent way to leave here, I thought.

Sundancer suddenly decided upon a memorial to him that he was sure Pam and Harmony would love to have ∼ something he thought they could find at the store and bring home. Little tinkling sounds filled my head which immediately brought my mind the two silver Chinese hand exercise balls I had in my living room.

I explained to Pam how they are about one inch in diameter, and that when they move they have the sweetest little tinkling sound. I suddenly realized that this was the sound that Harmony could hear, and in fact he acknowledged to us that it the silver ball sound was very similar.

Sundancer was pleased that I had something familiar that could create "his sound."

"You'll know it when you see it Mom. Go to that nature store," he blurted out joyously. And I've no doubt she did.

Our conversation began to draw to a close. Sundancer, Harmony and Pam had shared a very warm and enlightening conversation that would remain in their thoughts and hearts for a very long time. I felt privileged to have been a part of it.

As the old saying goes, "Time heals a broken heart," and time did its magic on Harmony and Pam, healing the grief felt at losing a good friend too soon. Today, years later, I still converse with them all. Harmony continues to maintain good health in spite of that serious, diagnosed condition; Sundancer still floats through conversations like a big yellow ball of energetic light; and Pam continues to consider herself fortunate to have them in her life, even if she can't pet one of them anymore.

"I know I'll be with him again one day, Colleen," Pam said at the end of one of our many conversations. "Just like I'll be with Coco and Muffit, and Daddy too. And even though some people think I'm nuts for feeling this way, I feel bad for them thinking that when something dies it's just the end. I believe they're missing out on something very wonderful ∼ very special ∼ and very uplifting, in spite of the initial sadness."

I agree with Pam. Life *is* an endless journey, a timeless trip with many bridges we all must cross. Death is only one of them, and its span is only as wide as our ability to perceive what's on the other side. ✑

Ming

"I see my sister. It is good to see her again, but I'm not near her yet. She has told me that I do not have to come back again like this, so I will take my time before I go...

"Thank you for being in my home, for the honour and respect that have always been mine, for the friends that you have given to me, for the dignity that you helped me maintain. Thank you for my solid (physical) life and know that I take you with me to my longer one (soul)."

These words began a message from Ming just hours before his body finally gave up and his vet helped him to cross over. It had been three years since he had almost died from kidney disease, three years more than they had expected to have with him.

As he spoke, he was showing me a beautiful, all-white cat with blue eyes wearing an electric-blue collar around her neck. I wasn't sure if blue was something she just wore in the world beyond ours into which Ming was about to enter, but Georgia remembered that Ming did indeed once have a white sister with blue eyes. She had died a few years before. It seemed that she had come to welcome him home.

I was fairly new to doing animal communications for the public the night I met Ming and his family for our first conversation. It was a night I will always remember, not for the conversation itself as much for the tremendous feelings of respect that they all had for one another. Ming was not just the family cat to this family; he was a genuine, intelligent, respected family member, holding no less importance than anyone else.

"Ming," Georgia would say, "is not a cat, he's a furry person, and he's my best friend in the world."

Although this in itself is not that rare, the fact that Ming felt the same way toward them amazed me. It was a mutual relationship, one hundred percent.

Living in the lap of feline luxury, Ming enjoyed a big house in the country, where every window he looked out of surrendered to him a beautiful scene. From back windows he could see the woods behind his home, where he could watch the local wildlife that Georgia eagerly feeds. The front windows issued forth a scene of rolling hills which were usually dotted with grazing thoroughbred horses. These views for a cat to ponder were a big yet welcomed change from Staten Island home they had recently moved from. And Ming seemed quite the contented and personable cat, appreciative of all life had to offer, in spite of his declining health.

Although he would be plagued with nightly hydrations on the kitchen counter, Georgia had once told me Ming would hop up there himself and wait on his towel for her.

"He'd stand there patiently, and he'd know when his treatment was just about over," she had said. "Then, when nearing his goal hydration point, he'd start to become a bit restless, as if to say, 'Okay, I'm all set now, Mom.' Then off he'd go in search of a place to relax, while he pondered some of life's mysteries. At his age, he seemed to have graduated from the playfulness some cats never tire of."

Georgia and Jim credited Ming's vet with doing a miraculous job at helping him keep a certain level of health as his kidneys failed over that three-year span. The most wonderful thing about it was that Ming maintained a good quality life. Despite blood tests and frequent veterinary visits, he never once resisted getting in the car to go, and never gave anyone at the vet's office a hard time either. He was truly a gentleman all the way.

At one point in our relationship, I was asked to help when Ming's friend Pasha suddenly became ill and died. Even though Ming was adored by Georgia's mom and dad, who lived with them in their house in a downstairs apartment, it was a sad time for him. He no longer had a companion, one of his own kind, to spend the days with while Georgia and Jim were at work. Even though Pasha had been a fearful cat, spending most of his time hiding, Ming really loved his buddy and would surely miss him. So, when Pasha crossed over Georgia thought that perhaps Ming should get some new feline friends to enjoy, friends that could help keep his grief to a minimum so that it would not overtake him and jeopardize what health he had held onto.

When Frosty and Smokey came to live with Ming it was quite a change in their household. Nothing like a baby to shake up routines, and two babies are even more unpredictable. From the start I figured that the "Project Manager" in Georgia, a position she holds in the real world, would be able to handle this with no problem; after all she is the most organized person I know. With her experience from Corporate America tucked under her fashionable belt, I figured she was an equal match for a couple of little kittens. However, everyone was in for a surprise ~ everyone but Ming, that is.

These two tiny balls of fur filled the house with activity and gave rise to many amazing tales. From the start, Smokey was the athlete. He spent his days dashing here and there, perfecting his muscle mass, of which he was quite proud, while Frosty, his petite and delicate sister, stuck like glue to Ming. She would sit and stare at him constantly, obviously intrigued by his majestic persona, rarely straying but never getting too close.

Instinctively the kittens understood that Ming was the unchallenged king of this pride. He got special treatment and special food, and the kittens never seemed to question this or feel left out. They knew that Ming was always fed first, and they would patiently await theirs. And Frosty seemed ever intrigued when Ming would get his evening hydrations, watching in awe from a distance. Even in the cat world, Ming was respected, and he in turn taught them much while looking down at the kittens as if he were a wise old lion who'd seen it all.

Georgia had made plans to retire in the fall, looking forward to spending the winter at home with her whole family instead of in another winter commute. In retirement, she hoped every morning could be like her Sunday mornings now, when she could turn on the stereo, crank up her old movie show tunes and dance through the house with a cat in arms ⁓ while Jim was out running errands, of course. However, Ming could not wait that long. He died on Memorial Day weekend. As hard as losing Ming was, this heart-breaking blow was softened some by the rest of the message he shared with us just shortly before crossing over:

> *"I will be here when your work is done and I will make new plans with you until fall. It is important for me to stay for you now and then to leave for Smokey. It will be his job to do as I did, and he will be very happy for the time and opportunity to be the wisest cat. Grandpa will tell you, 'Our Smokey is a very wise cat now, Georgi.' And Smokey will tell you important things, and he will tell Grandpa secret things. He won't be afraid to be the oldest cat anymore.*
>
> *"Frosty is my beautiful cat who I will always see. She will be a strong cat, stronger than she is now. You will always know that you can talk to Frosty and she will talk back. She will be Grandma's favorite girl and Frosty will give her many silent laughs.*
>
> *"My Daddy will miss me very much, but it will be with smiles. He will see me first when I return, and I will be with Pasha one more time.*
>
> *"This is a happy time ⁓ a time of wonderment and joy, a time of peacefulness and life, a time of giving back what we have received. Put it on my rock, Daddy. Put it on our Celebration Rock.*
>
> *"You have been my mother since you looked at me the first time. This picture is in my heart, too. Please sing to me. We are happiest when you sing your songs. There are no words here that I can say. Words are only shadows of what you are: my other Mother.*

"Dapple and gray,
Dogs that will bay...
Kittens that mew,
Cats that sing, too...
Horses of beauty,
Birds of great song...
Ming is not gone!
We are not alone...
Just Ming has gone home.

Ming of Donovan
The Happy Cat"

Ming's presence still is felt in the Donovan household, and when Georgia is enduring a difficult time, he is always there to offer his wisdom on the situation, which is always gratefully accepted.

Smokey has truly turned into the king of their pride, and Frosty is a strong cat, despite her sensitivity to the feelings of those around her. Bentley has joined the indoor crew, and although he resembles Ming in colouring and breed, he certainly is a different cat. As the "baby" of the family, even at three years old, now he's the most active and the most verbal, always looking for a good game of ball.

"I know that Ming will wait for me," she says, and I believe she is right.

New animal friends come and go through their lives, and whether they live indoors or out, each has their own special piece of Georgia's heart. Yet I believe that whether the animal friends be peanut- or panda-sized, Ming's piece will always remain the biggest.

I think of these things everytime I go to visit Georgia and Jim and the menagerie of animals they still share their lives with. Whether I look out over the rolling hills that are dotted with grazing thoroughbred horses, or I watch the wildlife feeding from the salad bar in the backyard that Georgia prepares daily for the woodchucks and others who come to visit, I always think of Ming. And always, before I leave, I bend down to touch his Celebration Rock, while in my own heart I celebrate in his honour, all who respect each other ∿ no matter the species ∿ no matter their place in life.✑

Pasha

*"I would like to be a big bird, and to soar like a hawk,
because hawks aren't afraid of what's on the ground."*

Many people find their life filled with love from a wonderful companion animal they brought home from "the pound." The reasons why these animals wound up there are usually varied and sad, but once adopted, most are able to shake off their questionable past to live a life of happiness with their new family.

For some, they never seem to fully recover from the unknown traumas that had shaped their life beforehand. So with these animals, it is even more special to hear that they finally did find humans who would love them, no matter what. This was the case with Pasha.

I wanted to share with you this story about a special little cat, who barely ever spoke. As Pasha was too shy to utter many words, our conversations were usually done with Georgia asking questions of Pasha, then Ming relaying Pasha's response. For this household, two interpreters were needed: Ming for Pasha, and me for the both of them. Because of this, my notes were always filled with words of wisdom from Ming: however, I rarely had more than a glimpse into Pasha's world. So, to share this story, I asked Georgia if she would share with me her notes from our conversations with the cats some years ago.

"I wanted a second cat, and a companion for Ming, after my Pumpernickel had passed away," Georgia wrote. "He was a blue-point Himalayan, like Ming, and I think that from the very start of his life, Pasha had not felt loved or wanted."

I remembered from our first conversation that Georgia had adopted Pasha from a shelter, after being urged by a friend of hers to go see this beautiful, purebred cat. When she arrived, she couldn't believe that such a beautiful cat would be abandoned at a shelter, so she made arrangements to bring Pasha home.

"All his life, he was not 'my cat,' she conveyed, explaining further how he and her dad, Papa, had bonded almost immediately.

"He spent most of his day under my parents' bed, in their apartment, which is in my home, and only came out to eat," she went on.

"He never came out when a stranger came to the house, and the sound of the doorbell or of the door opening up would send him scurrying under the bed. He would stay there until the stranger finally left. He did prowl the house every night though, like a vampire who only came out after dark," she teased.

Because of Pasha's fears, Georgia was never able to physically show him how much she loved him, because hugs and kisses were not his thing. But with her dad, it was different. Pasha was a good companion for Ming too, who enjoyed time with his apprehensive friend after dark, or by getting under the bed with Pasha to take a little nap. And when Georgia would call me to speak with the cats, it was usually Ming who spoke for Pasha, making sure that Pasha's wishes were always understood.

Early in life, Pasha developed urinary problems, and once required surgery to remove a blockage. Five years later, when the problem returned, he had to be rushed to the emergency room for immediate care.

Georgia had once explained that whenever Pasha went to the vet, he would just sit in his carrier and not make a sound. Having a stranger poke and prod, without him giving any resistance at all, seemed astounding.

On his last trip to the vet, Pasha was very ill. Tests showed very serious kidney and urinary problems, but Georgia was told surgery was not needed. With an unsure prognosis and medicine in hand, she took her friend home, where he seemed to hold his own for a few days before taking a turn for the worse. At this point he was admitted to the animal hospital.

Shortly after, Georgia called, and together we spoke with Pasha. As in many communications before, Pasha did not communicate directly to me, but rather to his friend Ming, who then made Pasha's wishes known.

Ming explained to us that Pasha felt he was too shy to ever endure what Ming did nightly with his routine fluid treatments aimed at treating his own kidney disease. Pasha simply couldn't imagine his personal space being invaded that way, on a regular basis.

Pasha made it clear that he had made a decision to leave now. His only regret conveyed to us was for not having had one more opportunity to look at Ming's face, or to say good-bye to Georgia's parents, because he knew they needed him in their lives.

Pasha went on to say that he wanted to be a big bird ∽ to soar like a hawk ∽ because a hawk isn't afraid of what's on the ground. Then he made reference to the "Meerkat," describing it as a guardian-angel cat, in heaven, who helps cats here when it's their time to cross over. She had spoken with him that very day, and she was ready to help him over to the other side of life.

The conversation took a turn and switched over to Ming, who was now telling us that Pasha was "a very sick boy." Concentrating on how this was affecting him now, and not his buddy, Ming asked if a picture of Pasha and himself could be put out for all to see, with a blue stone nearby. He went on to repeat that Pasha's only worry was for Momma and Papa, Georgia's elderly parents.

It was at this point, during the end of our conversation, that I clearly remember a change taking place.

"I don't know what it is, Georgia, but all of a sudden, everything feels very different," I told her. "I've never felt this before, but it's very uplifting, as if being swept upward. Pasha doesn't seem to be speaking anymore. I guess has conveyed all he wanted to say."

Marking the time in my appointment book as finished at 8 p.m., we said our good-byes and hung up the phone. I walked to the living room to be distracted from the sadness that I felt for Pasha's illness and his family, but I no sooner got there than the phone began to ring. At 8:05 p.m., I answered it, and could hear Georgia's voice on the other end. I could tell that she was crying now.

"Colleen, I just had to tell you that while we were finishing our call at 8 o'clock, Dr. Tom called on the other line and spoke with my husband, Jimmy. Pasha has passed away, and it just happened before he called to tell us."

It was clear to both Georgia and I that *this* was the change I had felt come over me, while we spoke in those final minutes of our call. It was a relief for Georgia, I think, to have been able to be with Pasha as he left this world for the next, and for me, it was an honour. Pasha clearly was not alone when he died.

Several days later, Jim saw an unexpected sight when looking out of the kitchen window toward the backyard. There was a huge hawk in the woods behind their house. As he watched, the hawk flew up and around the property, and then circled the house. The very next day it was on a tree near the house, where it stayed while Jim took its picture.

"I guess Pasha got his wish," she wrote at the end. "He got to soar like a fearless hawk."

I believe she was right.

Soon after, Papa planted a memorial tree in the backyard, and a stone with Pasha's name on it was set lovingly underneath. To this day, years later, whenever Papa is outside, he bends down to place a kiss from his fingertips upon Pasha's rock, and in my mind I can still here him say, "Oh, he was my good boy, alright."

Although the hawk has not been seen since, if not in the sky, we all believe that Pasha does still live on, surely, in each of their hearts. ✋

Kody

"The place I have come to
is the place you have helped make for me ..."

And, so began a message of soul-wrenching beauty,
from one many would consider an unlikely source.

Believing in Angels is a big thing today. Whether the volumes written are old or new, ancient or contemporary, whether written about them or supposedly by them, whether they are beautiful art books picturing them in their various splendor, books on Angels are in every bookstore across the country.

Throughout the ages, these heavenly hosts are accredited with miracles of all kinds, and the mere thought of them brings comfort into the hearts of most. As children, we are taught that Angels watch over us while we sleep, keeping us from harm. And although we can not see them, they are always there, guiding us through life, before accompanying us to heaven when we die.

As a child, I believed that Angels from heaven watched over animals, too. As an adult, I believe some of those Angels take human form, and I see one in my friend Susan. This story about her and her very special friend. His name is Kody, and he's a pig.

Against the beautiful backdrop of a 250-year-old farm in Buck's County, Pennsylvania, my good friend Susan spends her days tending to pigs. Potbelly pigs of all sizes dot the picturesque landscape, and Susan is fortunate to have her passion be her job.

Not only is she a highly reputable breeder of "pots," Susan is also a rescuer, a supplier of high-quality pig feed and supplies, an educator extraordinare, and consultant. Along with this, she also runs a boarding facility called "Ross Mill Farm and Piggy Camp," but all too often it could really be referred to as "Fat Camp," because many pigs are brought to Susan for help with obesity. Sad as it is, many, many people are far too ignorant to see the cruelty of feeding a pig more than it needs. In fact, this way many are literally *loved to death*.

Always putting the pigs first, Susan takes each one in and slowly helps them melt the fat off their chubby hams, while educating their people on how to best care for their beloved pet, keeping each pig's individuality in mind. Good fencing separates those that need separating, and the boarding pigs get a comfy spot of their own.

A herd in itself has healing qualities that humans only vaguely perceive, but pigs seem to thrive upon. With this understanding, Susan starts each day. Compassion is intertwined with reality, and she balances them both with elegant simplicity, as she stands amidst the pigs. The first time I visited her farm, it was in this vein that I first saw Susan's angelic wings.

"Can you see me, Suey? I can see you in there! How could they do this to you?" As she knelt by the fat pig's face, a pig who had once been her own, she first looked heartsick, then angry.

Suey's obese body lay on the floor of the vet's office as Susan pried open the fat rolls that had permanently squeezed his eyes shut. Not only was Suey fat-blind, but he was also dying. Such a simple thing as an ear infection had become closed off by rolls of fat, forcing the infection inward to his brain. Propped up with sandbags, not only did he live in a world of darkness and pain, he now was in unfamiliar surroundings without any comforts of his own. I was appalled.

Dr. Wilbers came in to check on him every hour or so. A strong man, he would pick Suey up, turn him over, then readjust his sandbags to help make him more comfortable. The rest of the time Suey stayed there alone. Never before had I seen anything like this and I recoiled in shock at the sight.

As Dr. Wilbers finished up, Susan settled back in along Suey's side.

"You're going to be alright, Suey," she half-shouted at the pig. "Do you hear me? It's going to be okay. I am with you," Susan said. Then I watched her wipe a tear away from under her glasses, and I choked back tears of my own.

As she pried open his eyes once more, cleaning more dirt and debris out from inside the rolls of fat, she took a deep breath and patted him on the hams before rising. I stood still, now halfway between disbelief and rage. How could anybody do this to an animal? More so, how could anyone do this to an animal they loved?

This is the picture of Susan that touches me the most ∽ huddled on her knees with the fat pigs who come to her farm ∽ while comforting them in their despair. As she pries open the eyes of each pig blinded by fat, hers is the first face they have seen in a long time, and they soon learn that she will not let them give up, nor will she give up on them, or any other pig who comes her way. Susan loves them all, and gives all she has to each. And so it seems they do see and hear her, even if they are not the fat pig she's tending to at the time ... even if they're only watching from the side-lines.

I hadn't heard from Susan for a few weeks after learning one of her older pigs, Kody, was ill. I knew that despite her valiant efforts to help him get well, he had continued to deteriorate, and things began to look grim. Sitting in front of my computer early that morning, my eyes locked onto the message I'd been waiting for. Reading Susan's carefully picked words describing Kody's illness, then his eventual crossing, my heart sank as I realized it had taken her two weeks before finding the inner strength to write this message to me.

She wrote of how she had eventually realized that Kody would not be getting better, so she had stopped annoying him with her medical efforts and instead spent all of the time she could just sitting and reading him poetry. Her grief made it quite evident how special Kody had been to her, and in turn, I was about to learn that she had been very special to him, as well.

With the first, unexpected words he spoke to me, to her, I knew I needed to record his message. Somehow I already knew that this was going to be monumental.

> *"The place I have come to is the place you have helped make for me, by helping me to understand and by reinforcing what Mother and the others had taught me as a small pig. This is a place of no coughs or diets, broken bones or broken hearts, heavy spirits or avenging angels ~ rather peaceful, graceful, soothing love. I am in a 'way station' at my choosing.*
>
> *"We always have a job in life, and being sure that I am still full of life, I have chosen the job of helping others realize what has happened to them when they arrive here. I will do this only for a while, until I decide to move on. I choose this because of all my herd who helped me while I was there. Did you know that you were in my herd?*
>
> *"I listened to you with my soft ears when you would talk to the fat pigs, and tell them to see you and be well. I listened to the fat pigs as they slowly started to talk again, because they realized that you would not give up on them. They were scared and frightened and lonely, but you were always there for them. They did not give up, because you did not give up. Pigs do not forget, and even Suey remembered that you were with him and what you said. I want to work like that, for a while, because this is good.*
>
> *"When any being lives through example, the Earth is a better place. Telling your people how you spent time with me will most assuredly ensure that another sick pig, whose time there has come to a close, will leave his heavy self while being caressed and loved and read poetry to. They will cross the bridge from one life to another filled with the knowing that they were important, their work was good, and that they will*

always remain on the winds of knowledge for their herd.

"All grow from each experience chosen and fulfilled. From the fat pig with no apparent choice in life, to the pampered pig with all desires met, to the abused pig without a chance to survive ∼ all of these choices were made with hopes to grow. And do you know what makes them more lovely? When they chance upon beings like you, beings who care, beings who try to help, and then cry when they feel they have failed.

"I would like you to know that there is no failure. Failure means that nothing was learned, nothing was gained. Failure means that nothing was even tried. There is always a lesson learned. There is always growth of some significant kind.

"When I first arrived here I was with light and love, the things you sent me here with. I was not frightened, as I knew this was my journey to another life. Some were not of the same knowing. Some were like the fat pigs whose people drop them off in a barn with no lovelies from their own home, into a herd that is not their own, with a dark world of wonderment and unanswered questions to fill their hearts. 'Why?' is what all of the fat pigs ask when they come to your farm.

"Here I want to work like you do. I want to help pry open their tightly closed eyes that are sad and fearful. I want to soothe them and say, 'See me! You are not alone.' I want to explain to them what is happening and that they are alright.

"And I want you to know that you have helped me to learn lessons and to grow. Before my life with you, I did not know these things. This is how I will now remain on the winds of my herd's Knowing.

"So, 'Do not weep at my grave ...' as we read in your storybook. Rather look at the sky, at the barn, at our herd ... Look at the people who come to you for help ... Look into the eyes of yet one more fat pig who can not see, and then look at

yourself and smile, knowing that you are learning too. There is growth. And all growth is good.
        Kody"

As I sat with tears streaming down my face and fingers trembling upon my keyboard, I finished a short, personal note of condolence to my friend Susan, before rereading Kody's message one last time. When reaching to hit SEND, I swear I felt a puff of piggy breath over my right shoulder. I took it as a sign of approval that I'd heard and translated well all he had wanted to convey.

While the letter traveled its short distance over the internet and into Susan's mailbox, I felt so honoured to have been a part of a message so magnificent. I swore to myself that day, that I would *always* remember that when I interact with one being, it does indeed affect others nearby. Not only does every deed we do go by quite noticed, the ripples in the pond of life extend far beyond what we imagined. ❧

Oreo

"Well, I needed to get over this, but I do not like to cry. I am still your good friend, but I don't have to be gross anymore."

Janet had called fairly regularly the year before Oreo died from cancer. It was a difficult time for her because she wanted to be very sure that she was doing the right thing for her little black-and-white friend with the treatments she chose, and the ones she let pass by. Her goal was to keep Oreo as healthy and happy as possible, prolonging a quality life, if not curing her altogether. And for a while, things went pretty well.

Oreo suffered a cancer the vet had explained as being aggressive and deadly. The only hope conventional medicine could offer was chemotherapy and amputation. These seemed such harsh choices to choose from for a beloved friend she'd shared her life with for so long. So Janet sought out Oreo's advice as to how they should proceed.

From the very beginning I remember Oreo being very clear about the fact that she did not consider herself ill at all. Surprised, Janet and I both inquired as to what Oreo's explanation was regarding the vet's interpretation of her health.

"I'm a happy cat," she kept repeating, and that was all she seemed to think mattered.

Oreo went on to discuss up front, and without much emotional attachment, how she did *not* want to lose her leg. She seemed a very proud kitty, who had always taken pride in her good grooming. To be without a leg seemed stupid and embarrassing to her. Janet took her friends wishes and tried to work with them.

Over the coming months, Janet tried various holistic approaches to help Oreo regain the kind of health that Oreo, herself, insisted she already had. As the months stretched toward the year mark, it became evident that the vet's diagnosis of cancer did seem to be accurate and that the approaches Janet had been trying were not working as she had hoped.

An ulcer appeared on the leg where the cancer had been diagnosed. It developed into an unsightly sore, and Oreo began to "look" sick, and lose weight. from refusing to eat. However, she maintained that she was not going to die, and that Janet needn't think of euthanasia right then.

Just before Christmas, Janet's mother suddenly died, forcing her to leave Oreo in the care of close friends while she traveled to Arizona to tend to her mother's funeral and estate, not to mention Abby, her mom's only cat. Emotionally drained by now, Janet worried not only about Oreo, who needed her at home, but also her mother's cherished cat who had just been orphaned.

Calling me once from Arizona to communicate with Oreo at home, Janet conveyed her concerns over everything to her, asking her if she would mind awfully if Abby came home with her. Janet didn't want to do anything to compromise Oreo any further, and she knew that this would be asking a lot from her sick and weak friend.

Oreo seemed to sympathize with Abby's sad situation, and agreed that bringing Abby to their house would be a very nice thing to do. Then she laid out some ground rules she asked to be followed. Although Abby seemed to her a very sweet, loving cat, Oreo was concerned about getting bumped or by just having to see her much once they returned. Oreo felt too weak to want to deal with it. Janet understood completely and agreed to Oreo's terms. She arrived back home a week or two later.

Abby tried to settle in, but hid a lot during the evening. Oreo began to rally at first, but then steadily began to slide downhill. A month later, she passed away.

Devastated, Janet called to tell me Oreo was gone, and I comforted her as best I could. Knowing there was really nothing I could do for her right then, except listen, I did. Soon after, Oreo began to speak, and her message came through with the same clarity as did our first conversation. She felt strong, full of life, and with a conviction that she was still just fine. I began to type.

"Did you know that I can see what you can not see now? It's true! I can see that sometimes a cat just has to move on, even though she was pretty happy in fur. It's okay to do this, Mom. You can do it too, when it's your turn. You don't have to be sad or scared. Just be practical and it will work out fine.

"You know, we had lots of nice times, you and me, just like you had lots of nice times with your mom. Abby had lots of nice times with her too. It's just part of the beautiful plan of 'life.' And in this you will know that I am here to await your return, like your mom is for you, and she was for me. And we both will be waiting when it's Abby's time. Isn't that the best? It's the way it has always been, and the way it will continue to be.

"Those of the heart always live on. When you talk about me, I'm more than a memory. So don't be sad for too long ⁓ I still live on, because you love me, and because I am real. And, even here, I am still a happy cat, the one you called Oreo.

"I love you, Mom ⁓ always.

Oreo"

While Abby continues to settle in, getting used to living without the loved one she lost, Janet confides that she has found some peace of her own, too. Oreo lived her life here on her own terms, and her message solidifies Janet's belief that she does indeed live on.

If only all could find more solace like this when faced with life's cruelties. However, I often contend that even within the darkest cloud life can send our way, there is always some sliver of silver lining to be found, if we just take the time to look. ❧

Morgan

***"Here I am, Momma! I can see you and PK and Casey
and Cookie, too. I can see everyone here and there!"***

At 17 years old, Morgan was sight for sore eyes. A gray, long-haired cat, she looked a fright, with her matted fur and skinny body. Morgan had bumps along her spine that were extremely painful to the touch, so grooming could not help her look more tidy. Spending most of her latter days on a table, where she wouldn't be bumped by the four large dogs she lived with, Morgan was actually a very contented cat. With her feline companions, Murphy, Shaggy and Casey, she was a happy cat, even though an outsider might have trouble believing this.

Where Morgan now resided, in the meadow before the Rainbow Bridge, are the many cats with whom she had shared this lifetime. You see, when I first met Joyce, she had fourteen cats! Of those who have crossed over to the next stage of life, many were old, many had suffered an unexplained kidney disease at a relatively early age, one had suffered a tragic vaccine reaction and one simply did not want to be here. Morgan and Joyce and all the others had suffered the loss of many loved ones in only a four- or five year-span.

Morgan's first words from her new perspective were joyous and excited, reassuring Joyce that the stage of life we call death was not a final curtain. The rest that followed was warm and tender, and showed that the best part of us always survives.

"I know you were sad for me, but I am here," she exalted. "This is just fine with me. It was time."

The joy in Morgan's expressions felt liberating and vast.

"Did you know that I am the Most Beautiful Cat now?" she asked. "PK even told me this. It is wonderful to not have a broken down body anymore. I sure kept it for a long time, didn't I?

"Do you remember when I was a smaller cat and had beautiful fur? I have that now," she confided in a manner that made us both giggle.

"Do you remember when I had bumps on my spine?" she also asked, but she did not give Joyce even a millisecond with which to respond. "I don't have them anymore," she chortled.

The most soothing message a grieving person can ever hear is probably the one where they are told that their lost loved one will wait for them. The belief that seeing them again one fine day is the only thing that gets some through the grieving process and on with their lives. For my friend Joyce, this was also so.

Having lived with so many animals in her life, and having cried so many tears when each one had died, Joyce had finally come to the conclusion that it didn't matter to her if she never saw them again. Of course she hoped that wouldn't be the case, but if it was, that would be okay.

"I love them while they're here," she once told me when I asked her to remember Morgan with me while writing this book. "Really, that's the most important thing to me, and I know they love me, too. I don't want them to feel that they need to wait for me before continuing on with their lives," she said before pausing for a few moments, trying to form her words so they'd reflect her true feelings.

"I'm not afraid anymore, to open my heart to another animal after losing a longtime companion," she resumed. "There was a time when I did feel that way, and it was a very sad place for me to be."

"I know I'll see many of them again one day, maybe here, maybe there," Joyce said, her voice sounding strong with conviction. "In the meantime, I know we shared something very special. Knowing there is a life for them, after they leave here, has helped me more than words can express."

I agreed, and thought about my own three sleeping pigs in the room outside my door. Before I knew about animal communication, and before I heard from the animals themselves what life meant to them, through their eyes, I too, was completely devastated when one would die.

What the animals have taught me is that life is not something which ends when we shed our bodies. There is a far greater purpose to our life than just what's here on Earth, and a far greater place which we ascend to when we leave.

When the time comes when one of our pigs decides they will be the first to move on, I know I'll be lost in grief, for a while, but only for missing their physical presence. I know in my heart that when my emotions subside, I will hear them, if I listen, and any message they may wish to send me from their new home … that place we all come from … that place where we all return.

It doesn't really matter if they have a body that I can pat and caress, even though I cherish each moment that I can. I know that they, like Morgan, each have a Soul that lives forever. I'm sure we are not accidents happening in each other's lives, rather we are lessons, both planned and executed. And I believe I will carry them with me, throughout time and space, within that part of me which lives forever. I only hope that they will carry a part of me with them, too.

I'm thankful for the animals in my life, as Joyce is with hers, and my other clients are with theirs. It's through the animals that I have learned so much about the true nature of life. And I believe I am a better person because of them. ⌘

Sometimes they wait...

Chapter 9

Avalanche

"I fooled you, didn't I?" she said.

Unassuming and wrapped in joy, these were the words my spotted friend told me during her first conversation from the other side of life. Smiling at the mere thought of Avalanche actually wanting to speak, because she was never much of a conversationalist, I wiped a tear from my eyes. I had just learned that a good friend crossed over to Rainbow Bridge, and I hadn't picked up on this possibility before.

Given a name that tried to depict her uniqueness, and unique she was, Avalanche was born at a nearby home, under some potentially disastrous conditions, Joyce had told me.

It was a typical midwinter day in central New York. Outdoors the snow flew while being whipped by the frigid wind, and temperatures hovered in the teens. Yet, despite the inhospitable world outside, a litter of beautiful, healthy pups was delivered in the warmth of a home with family nearby. Unlike strays and homeless animals who spend life braving the weather's worst elements, these puppies were fortunate to have come into the world in such gracious surroundings.

After the puppies were born, their mother got up, went to the door and asked to go outside. The door was opened, out she went and then her people returned their full attention back on the whelping box, which was now full of tiny white pups.

Before long, the familiar sound of a dog wanting in was heard at the door. Someone hurried to let the new mother hustle in out of terrible cold. Just as the door was closing behind the dog, something caught their eye. Stopping the door in mid-swing, they strained their eyes to make out what it was that had grabbed their attention. Through the blowing, swirling snow, the image finally came into focus: right outside the door was one last little white pup. Avalanche was born in a snowbank.

I met Avalanche when she was about five years old. We were instant friends. She was the first Dalmatian I had ever known, and that in itself will always keep her special to me.

Avalanche was a high-strung dog, as I soon learned was common for her breed. Also common is the need for keeping a good eye on a Dalmatian's diet, because they have a tendency to blimp out easily.

Thoroughly entranced by the moment, I reached down to pet her ears. Instantly she cried out and backed away.

"Oh, it's not your fault, Colleen," Joyce told me as I apologized to her faithful friend. "She's done that ever since a she was a puppy."

"It's okay, Avalanche," she squatted and told the dog. "Colleen didn't know."

Joyce patted Avalanche on the rump as the spotted wonder bounced around the kitchen. It was the dogs' and cats' dinnertime, and Avalanche had spied a piece of broccoli ∼ something she always went crazy for, and something I have since come to suspect is purely a Dalmatian thing.

Feeling bad for having made her cry, I promised Avalanche that I would never do that again. I knew as I spoke though that it would always be hard to resist the urge to pet those lovely speckled ears. And as time went by, I came to believe that Avalanche's tender ears must have come from being born in a snowbank. Perhaps they'd never gotten over the shock of the bitter cold "blanket" she was delivered into.

Healthy and very active, Avalanche spent her days bopping around with her best friend, Freeway, a dog Joyce had rescued from a junkyard years before. Ever since she'd come to live with them as a puppy, Avalanche was most attached to him ～ practically at the hip.

"Freeway really loves her," Joyce told me one day, confiding that she'd always believed she came second in Avalanche's life. She told me too that it was understandable to her. As she said, "Freeway is a pretty magnificent guy."

"He took it upon himself to raise Avalanche," Joyce went on to say. "Maybe because she was so young when she came here? I don't know. But he has always watched out for her, and she minds him well."

So from the very beginning, Freeway always watched out for his spotted friend, even when she was flitting about in a seemingly uncontrollable, joyous state. A state otherwise known as "Avalanche's everyday state."

When Freeway passed away in December of 1995, Avalanche was lost, heartbroken. Devastated without her buddy, she moped around the house and was obviously in deep grief. The other dogs in the house were not enough to fill the void in her. They could not fill his place in her heart or her life, and it was clear to see that a part of her died too.

For the rest of her life, Avalanche would picture Freeway often whenever she would converse with me, and for her, conversations were mostly done with pictures and feelings. Although her grief lessened over time, as grief always does, Avalanche would still send me feelings of loneliness whenever Freeway was mentioned.

In March 1998, after 13 years of never being sick, Avalanche suddenly became ill. Her face started to swell and she had trouble eating and drinking. Her life-long vet tried various approaches to help her, as did Joyce with holistic therapies, but progress was very slow and questionable.

On April 23, without help, Avalanche crossed over and another long era in Joyce's life came to an end. Or did it? Before driving even a few blocks from the vet's office, on her way home after Avalanche's sudden crossing, Joyce was sure she heard her dog speaking.

"I'm here, Mom! I'm okay," the voice said joyfully.

Wiping her eyes, Joyce debated with herself over what she'd just heard. Had her newly departed dog just spoken to her from heaven, or was it merely wishful thinking?   She wasn't sure.

I am always amazed at the supposed coincidences in life. I was at a writing class the evening Avalanche died. My teacher had just found out that I was working on this book, and asked if I would share part of it with her. Reaching for the manuscript, I flipped back and forth through the many stories it contained, and after the third time of coming back to it ∽ the pages falling open to this spot as if for a reason ∽ I pulled out Freeway's story.

Glancing at the clock to see how late it was, I handed the story to her at 9:25 p.m. This wouldn't take her too long to read and then I'd be on my way, I thought. She read, I hurried home, and upon my arrival I had word of Avalanche's death.

Slowly I walked to the phone to call Joyce, my mind poring over the conversation we'd had earlier that day. It was only a few hours before, just as I was getting ready to leave for class. Although Joyce had been worried because Avalanche was having new, labored breathing, I was confident that Avalanche wasn't contemplating crossing over. How could I have missed something this big?

Joyce told me how after we had spoken, she searched for a vet who would see Avalanche that night, because theirs was too far away and unable to get back in reasonable time. Finally finding one that would squeeze them in, off she went with her spotted friend in search of some kind of medical help. The news was not good.

X-rays showed that Avalanche was dying of congestive heart failure, something that had come on in just a few days, since the last time she had seen her regular vet. Because of her age, nothing invasive was decided upon, and she began to deteriorate quickly. Joyce told me it was plain to see that Avalanche would not last the night.

Finishing her story by telling me what she'd heard in the car on her way home, she wiped her eyes once more. Thinking back to just before Avalanche had taken her last breath, Joyce said, "I told her to go, Colleen. I told her, 'Go with Freeway'."

Avalanche died somewhere between 9:20 and 9:30 p.m., at the same time I was compelled to pull Freeway's story out for someone new to read.

I was apologizing to my friend for not realizing this crossing was imminent when I was startled to suddenly hear Avalanche speak to me.

"I fooled you, didn't I?" Avalanche suddenly blurted out exuberantly. I sat in amazement, my jaw hanging open and surely causing me to look silly.

"It's okay, Colleen," Joyce reassured me. "I didn't feel she was this critical either."

In between bouncing about like a puppy, Avalanche tried to focus her thoughts on us. She offered her red coat to Jill, one of her doggy friends she left behind at home. Days before she did not want to share, even in thought, any of her possessions, but now she seemed to realize that material things weren't important anymore.

"Oh, Mom, and when my ashes come home, could you put them in the same can as Freeway's?" Avalanche innocently asked.

She seemed to get the message quickly that this was a somewhat unappealing idea for Joyce. In an instant, before Joyce even had a chance to formulate a response to the question put before her, Avalanche decisively rephrased her request.

"Okay, can you tape them together?" she queried.

Since it was late of hour, and very difficult for me to keep up with Avalanche's joyous bouncing about the ethers, we all agreed to talk more the next day. Avalanche assured me she would have more to say, but right then she didn't really want to talk anymore. Staying true to form as a minimal conversationalist, Joyce and I laughed at the thought, because the few words she had already uttered were certainly memorable ones.

Without a word, Freeway quietly appeared before me and I could see a look of contentment on his old familiar face. Avalanche snuggled up to his side.

As the pictures faded from view, Joyce and I hung up our phones, both reflecting on the range of emotions experienced that night, and more so, on how long Avalanche had waited to see her most favorite friend again. We could certainly wait to speak with her another day, knowing she'd arrived at her destination in good stead and good company. As of this writing, we still are waiting.

From time to time, through the years since her death, I've caught glimpses of Avalanche bouncing around heaven, as if in uncontrollable joy. Freeway is always nearby. And although she has never taken the time to really discuss her life and plans, only offering a quick thought or fleeting picture here and there, that's okay with Joyce because it really doesn't matter anymore. The comforting thing is knowing that Freeway and Avalanche are no longer apart ∼ they have crossed the Rainbow Bridge together. ❧

Sometimes they come back...

Chapter 10

Samson

"You will see me. Then you will be happy, because you will see me again ∽ your big, black cat."

The first consultation I had with Samson and his human mom, MaryLea, came as a sympathy gift from a close friend of hers who had arranged the appointment for her. In his younger days, Samson was a big, muscular, jet black cat, who had always taken great pride in his athletic abilities. Recently he had crossed over after a long, debilitating illness, and MaryLea was having a difficult time grieving the loss of her good friend.

From the start, it was quite clear to me that Samson was not only alive and well, he was very happy, too. Even though he worried about MaryLea, who still couldn't control her tears, he wanted her to know he was just fine. He told me he still frequented her house, and she agreed that she could "feel" her friend in all of the places he told me he would visit. Samson also wanted MaryLea to remember she still had Tiffany, her other companion cat, who needed her loving attention as well.

Communications with Samson continued over the next few months as MaryLea learned to live without the physical presence of her longtime friend. Then, about five months after we first spoke, Samson revealed that he had made plans to return to a physical body.

"He's showing me a large, wild bobcat," I told her. "It seems like it lives in the mountainous region where North Carolina and Tennessee meet."

I don't know how I knew the terrain, as my geography is not very good, but MaryLea confirmed that this is indeed accurate for that region.

"The wildcat he is showing me is a pregnant female," I continued. "Samson is planning on becoming one of her kits!"

Astonished as I was, MaryLea was speechless. My thoughts jumped to how extraordinary this was ∼ to be able to communicate with a being who was consciously making plans for a new life experience in the physical world again. This was definitely a first for me.

For MaryLea, the news came with mixed emotions. Of course she wished her friend a wonderful life, wherever that would take him, but this was so soon after losing him and it was hard to accept that he was not returning to her. Only recently had she learned to cope better but still mourned his loss each day. I found her feelings quite understandable, and we both sat in silence for a few moments as Samson's message, and all of its ramifications, began to sink in.

I had never spoken with an animal once it returned to our world from the nonphysical, and I was quite amazed that this was happening so quickly. I had great reservations about how long these conversations could or would continue, wondering if they would be shut down the moment the wildcat delivered her kits. Only time would tell, and from my memories now, it seems it was only a few weeks later that Samson spoke to me as one of five or six baby wildcats newly born near the Appalachian Trail.

"I am special to my mother, because I am all black. She calls me Blackie," he said. Wrapped in a feeling of damp warmth, I began to feel many sensations as Samson spoke to me from his new body. It was very dark and I could not see a thing. Now and then I was nudged slightly, and the smell of earth and moss was very strong in my nose. I could feel the softest of warm fur against me, and I had a sticky feeling about my face which I quickly assumed was from milk. With a satisfied feeling in my stomach, I felt peaceful wedged in among Blackie's littermates.

My body felt very odd. Although it seemed I had no muscle control at all, there was a great strength that welled within me. I could feel his mother's breathing pattern, the low-toned thumping of her heart, and the most intense smell of her, which I could not possibly describe in human words. From what I could gather, Blackie felt like he was only a few days old. And in this peaceful, quiet environment, which I now found myself experiencing through him, I could feel an alertness never felt before while speaking with other cats.

This was all so different, new, and thrilling, and a great honor, as well. It was an experience I may have trouble putting to words, but one I will never forget. MaryLea and I ended the conversation when Blackie asked to go to sleep.

"Goodnight, Samson," she began to say, as she bid her old friend a good rest. "Oh, I mean good-night, Blackie."

Our few conversations afterwards were usually very short. The older Blackie got, the harder it was to connect with him. It was apparent to me that he was becoming solidified in this new experience and his old world, the one with memories of MaryLea, was being left behind, as it should be.

As a newborn, he communicated most often by feelings ∼ the way most baby animals I have conversed with do. As he grew older, I was able to see what he was showing me. I often wondered if that was because his eyes were now open and he could see physically. He spoke of the things his mother was teaching them, and he told us how famous he was going to be.

"I am very special. You will read about me in the newspaper," he said confidently one day. He was sure that his fame would come because he is all black and that was not common for his breed.

I am not familiar with the different kinds of cats in the world, but I believed Blackie knew what he was talking about. Although his new family looked like bobcats to me, I have to admit that my first instincts upon "seeing" his new little self, was that he was a panther.

As we approached the five-week mark, Blackie became difficult to reach. Up to that point, I could usually establish a good link with him during times when he would have been sleeping. He would show me images of himself playing with his littermates, his mother washing him and the feeling of learning to jump in the tall grass.

I would feel the coolness of the evening air on my face, and the wetness of the morning grass on my feet. I could smell their den and almost experience the incredible muscles he was learning to work with and make strong. I remember too one of the last things he conveyed to us: that we should watch for him on the news.

"You will see me. Then you will be happy, because you will see me again ⁓ your big, black cat," he said, and my conversations with MaryLea, regarding Samson, ended.

In the time since, MaryLea focused her much-needed attention on Tiffany, where a deeper bond was forged between the two. For a long time we both kept our eye on the news coverage, those last few minutes when they tend to air special, strange or odd occurrences.

Neither one of us ever saw mention of a black bobcat in our local media coverage, but that didn't matter. Some things the animals say don't pan out. Just like it is with humans. But one thing I'm sure of, without a doubt, is that Samson, now reborn as Blackie, is a very fast cat, just like he'd once been, while living in a house, in a city, in New Jersey. ✜

Always, there's a message …

Life goes on.

Chapter 11

Melvin the Large

"Angels, to a pig, are little beings who bring you food and make you feel nice. My mother told me that angels are not always pigs … that sometimes they are people or birds or 'see-throughs'. Mother also told me that I would never have to be frightened of the beings called Angels, and although I know it is a human word, it is a concept all pigs know. 'Angels are an unusual gift, and we all get at least one,' she said. I am glad my mother told me about these angels.

"I was born to live my life with humans. It was the job of all my herd to be animals of this kind. I expected this, and so it was, but as a piglet, I did not know what kind of life this would be.

"In my earlier days, I was loved with food. My people liked to feed me way too much. Being a pig, I was happy to let them. I ate candy and bread, leftover people food and things I found in my pen. When I got too big to move around much, they would bang things to make noise. I didn't like that noise, but I did move. For some reason, moving was not my thing to do.

"When I couldn't see any more, they would push me around, shoving me here and poking me there. I got mad about the way they treated me, so I would squeal, and they would laugh, poking me some more. It was frightening because I couldn't see them coming, but I could always find my food.

217

"I was never meant to stay long with those
people, I'm sure. I was a pig to help them learn about a kind
life. I was all alone in my pen, as I had no herd. In a world I
couldn't see, another pig would have been nice to have around,
but that was not the plan for me.

"My people said they couldn't eat me. This was good,
because I did not want to be eaten. They made me a big crate,
building some of it around me, then shoved me up onto a truck
and the wind blew my bristles all over.

"I came to a place that I learned to call home. It was
different than what I was used to ⁓ it had pigs, and grass ⁓
it had angels. I know, because they brought me food and made
me feel nice, even though I couldn't see them.

"My favorite angel came for me every day. She would
call me when she came, and I heard her, even though my ears
could not hear. I knew she was there, but I still acted frightened. I'm not sure why, but I think because it was new.

"My angel brought me food that was soft and warm,
and easy to eat. I had never had such food before but I decided
to like it because bread and candy didn't come. And I would
walk every day, with my angel beside me.

"I lived a long time there, it seems to me. Other people would come to see me, then leave, but she was always
there. One day, when she went away, I cried on the inside
because I had thought she would stay with me always. I did
not like my food being brought by another. I missed the pictures she showed me when we would be near, and I wondered
why she left.

"Another pig told me that his human does this sometimes, but not to worry because she always came back. He
told me too, to look for her in my memories, because it would
hurry her along and we would see her again sooner. But a pig
like me doesn't really like change, and he only spoke about his
human. My situation was different.

"So I decided to go find her on my own, which I did,

but when I found her she was crying inside, like I had been. She felt so alone and far away from herself, so I tried to tell her I was near. Surely she could see me because I am still a big pig, but she didn't seem to realize that I was standing right there ... Then I realized why ... I am a 'see-through' ... and I don't know how this happened!

"I looked myself over and do you know what I saw? Me. I look like the shadow under a tree. I have bristles and hooves, a straight tail and big snout, but I'm not hungry, I don't walk much ⌒ just arrive, and I can see really well with these eyes! This is a very nice feeling to me, but I think it has caused my angel to cry.

"I hear a sound on the far, distant wind. It calls to me. It calls out 'Melllvvviiin.'

"I turn back towards my angel who still cries inside. Though her ears do not work well, I tell her still, 'I am here, and I will stay. Even though the wind calls my name, I won't go. I will walk there later, when you can see me again. I will walk there later, by your side.'

"Now, while I wait, I'm beginning to realize many things...

"When I was blind and alone, it was given to me, a gift of my own ... I was given an angel my blind eyes could see. When I was unable to move on my own, and wouldn't get up without poking or shoving, I was sent far away, where angels could say that while I was there I walked peacefully each day. When I felt there was no love or kindness for me, my angel came forth and comforted me. In the days of my life when I lived with her near, I knew Mother was right ... angels were there.

"I don't want there to be tears of my life as a big pig. I lived like I should have ⌒ I was the best pig I could be. I learned that the angels do watch over me. This gift I was given I want to give back, and I'll walk by her side, like she once did mine, even though I'll be here, a 'see-through' of this

kind. Now I am her angel of a very large size.

"And the tears we've both shed for ourselves and each other float out into heaven where all stories began, where animals first came from, along with humans. We're a beautiful story that has no real end. We're a beautiful story of how love never ends.

Melvin the Large lived the last 10 months of his physical life surrounded by beauty he could not see, comfort like he'd never known, other pigs like himself, and a doting, loving human. Though miles were between them when he died, they were not there by choice, and I never believed they were his reason for dying.

Once abused with food, his obese body was probably more than his heart could endure. And although he lost pounds in the months spent at his new home, his spirit grew. Despite being blinded, deafened and crippled by the tremendous fat his spirit was enveloped in, Melvin was a very special pig. It won't be the lack of his big, fat body that will make the hole in his herd seem larger, rather it will be the loss of his great big spirit ∽ the one that saw angels with his inner eyes.

I shall never forget my friend, Melvin the Large, as I watch for his "see-through" hoof-prints beside Carol. ⟡

Sometimes it's forever …

Chapter 12

Arturo

"A goat will follow you to the ends of the Earth, but if you chase them, you'll chase him to the ends of the Earth,"
Kathy once told me. Those words were to have more meaning than I ever expected.

"Hello, Colleen? You don't know me but I was given your name by a friend I asked about animal communicating and I would *love* to have you talk to my goats for me."

This was how I met Kathy Hill. She was getting ready to move from the city to a home in the country, and she not only wanted to tell the goats about it, but also to ask the stray cats around her apartment if any of them would like to come along. Kathy had used animal communicators before, and it was fun speaking for the first time to animals who were used to communicating before me. Right away they were there and ready to talk, especially Arturo, her oldest of two goats.

Through the years and much communicating, Kathy and I became friends. I visited her new country home and walked the property with her and the goats as a "feel" was gotten for their new area. Arturo pointed out little woodland fairies and even a little fairy ring, which he refused to enter. This was interesting to me, because Arturo went everywhere else there was to go. He roamed their property daily, but the fairy ring was a sacred thing even to this goat. Quite proud of his long beard, which I always admired when I was with him, he told me how the fairies would tickle him in it.

When I think back to all of my experiences with Kathy and Arturo, I am always struck by what a dignified guy he was and how Kathy always boasted of his greatness to the world. They were fast friends, joined by more than a feed bucket, and I consider myself fortunate for having been their friend as well.

Dignity was a most important aspect of Arturo's personality. Of course he was funny, always having some pretty great things to say, and he could make a good joke, but Arturo's great dignity is what always stood out for all to see.

Toward the end of his life here, he spoke about a big rock that he wanted Kathy to get and put on the hill between the house and the barn. It was to be a memorial to him and she should plant flowers, "the kinds goats can eat."

"In the spring," he said to her, "you should spend some days out in that sunny spot where the goat flowers will soon grow." Then Arturo showed me pictures of this special spot-to-be, with Kathy sipping Bully Hill's "Love My Goat" wine while carving with hammer and chisel: *Arturo ~ The Greatest Goat of All.*

The last time I spoke with Arturo while he was in a physical body was the day that he asked for the vet to come to help him over.

"If I can't do it myself tonight, can the vet come in the morning?"

My heart sank, along with Kathy's. It was a hard thing to hear, but it did make sense. Arturo had been sick for two months. He'd been treated medically and homeopathically, prepared all kinds of special foods for, sat with, fussed on and read to, all in the hope of nursing him back to health. And all through that, he hadn't decided whether he was going to go yet.

Then one day, while Kathy was at work, Arturo had gone down, tipping the water bucket and getting his head stuck. Apparently, he had thrashed about for quite a while, based on the few little spots where he had rubbed off fur trying to get up. Once Kathy rescued him from his bucket and the position he'd gotten himself into, she called me to ask him what she should do.

It was clear from the start that Arturo was a changed goat. At some point in time that day, in the privacy of his own barn, as he struggled to get up and out of that bucket, Arturo lost more than a bit of fur off his chin ∼ he lost his dignity. Having Kathy find him that way was even worse. So on this day Arturo finally decided. He voiced his wishes, and Kathy spent one last night with her longtime buddy. The vet came the next morning.

The rest of this story is spoken from my two friends Kathy and Arturo. Kathy wrote the following tribute for a goat memorial web site. Following it is a story that I wanted to end this book with. It is a story from Arturo, his first message from his new vantage point on the other side of life. I want to share these with you as a final tribute, not just to a woman and her goat, but to all beings who share a bond that transcends time and space.

What the animals have taught me most, is that death is only an illusion, and that this is the greatest truth of all.

Arturo (1984-1998)

"Arturo came to me when he was about two months old, and everyone could see he was a special boy right from the start. He was always amiable and interested in whatever you were doing, and he had some great tricks. When he was little, if you bent down, he'd hop on your back for piggyback rides, looking all around and staying as long as you'd let him. He seemed surprised one day to be too big anymore, standing on me expectantly as I lay flat in the dirt after bending over to pick something up.

"He could turn on any light and open any bolted gate, and had half convinced me that he could fly, until one night when he let me in on his secret. He leapt up onto the stall wall, walked along with his hooves single-file, twisted his body around the post and onto the open gate, teetered along it, balancing his weight to keep it from swaying, and reached up to the ceiling to pull a two-inch light-bulb chain with his lips. He taught me a lot about goats that night.

"Arturo had an innate graciousness, one that usually surprised people who had 'heard about goats.' He was more polite than even many people seem to be anymore. He was a natural at parties. At a big family gathering, he sat among groups of people in the yard, and when anyone announced they were leaving, would get up, escort them to their car, then come back to the group. Each time he was followed by his herd-mate and his two worshipful ducks, so the whole gang got credit for it. It was a pretty hard procession to ignore.

"One night we were having a veggie cookout on the upstairs deck, and each time the doorbell rang, I'd run down to greet the latest arrival. When only one more person was due and the bell rang, everyone said, 'That's Mark.' I ran down and opened the door ～ and there stood Arturo with his herdmate, smiling expectantly at the thought of coming up for some veggies. (They waited, but got their share.) They rang that bell all throughout the party and some more the next day, and never before or since.

"If you read stories to him, he'd rest his head on your shoulder and look at the pictures.

"Arturo and I were close even in silence, always 'outstanding in our fields' (in good weather). But our relationship was incredibly en-riched over our last few years together by professional animal communi-cator Colleen Nicholson. Just like with Arturo, it started out as one of those little introductions you want to look back at later and marvel at for all it brought about.

"Outstanding in her own field as well, Colleen can not only clarify what our animal friends want and don't want, what they need and don't need, she's also able to communicate that sense of joy in being alive that animals feel, and that people often forget. She helped us each meet on our own terms, to stay open to possibilities, and to get each other's jokes.

"Arturo died on January 7, 1998. He was thirteen, though he'd had very few 'old' days. He'd gone sledding (he'd climb up the hill with you and run behind) and played a lot with kids in the snow for days, just days before he asked for the vet to come one last time. He was very calm and affectionate to the last, clearly content and appreciative of a life well-lived.

"Since he died at the end of a week-long thaw, we were able to have Arturo's body buried in the yard with a backhoe. In the spring, I'm going to get a big rock from the highway department to put over it, something suitable for engraving and future games of King of the Hill.

"The vet was surprised that, toward the end and weakened, Arturo made it a point to see him to his car, all on his own. That was him, all right. Arturo ⌣ the Greatest Goat of All."

(Reprinted with permission.)

Arturo's Message:

"Hey! Hello!! It's me, Arturo ⌣ the Greatest Goat of All!"

"Sorry that I have been taking so long to make my grand statement from over here, but I've had many things to do and I wanted to give you a detailed report. Of course, it hasn't really been very long, but Colleen is telling me that it is about three weeks or so. There's no more "time to fly." Isn't that funny?!"

"So here is my truth … the Truth of Arturo as told to you by myself through Colleen." (indicating to me that he hopes I can get this all right.)

"In the realm of who we are and where we come from, it is important to keep in mind that we must also remember where we wish to go. That's a lot of directions, isn't it? Rightly so, and this is why:

"As soon as I woke up in this body here, from my new, grand perspective I have remembered why I wanted to come to live with Kathy Hill. Well, I remembered that I wanted to be a goat of great distinction. This is something that I had been trying to achieve for a very long time, many lifetimes there, in that space, many times not being as successful as I had hoped to be. You see, I was oftentimes a goat or sheep, but

ones that lived far away in the mountains or on the hills of a lonely place. They were beautiful, of course, with many other species, and existence offered many lessons and worldly things to enjoy. But I, Arturo, wanted to experience something more than just that. I wanted to seek out an existence that offered experiences with the upright animals as well …

"One time, in another life, I met an old shepherd boy. He wore tattered cloth about his body and smelled of many odd things. He had long hair that was matted and white trailing down his back, but on top of his head he was shiny. He had a long white beard that traveled far down his body and he had only two feet for walking. He had eyes with a knowing of their own.

"He had been in the hills with his flock for a very long time, so the goats and sheep had told me. A small fire pit was there and a pile of branches that he slept under, as it seems that he was not as warm as we animals were at night., perhaps because he was all alone. And when I happened upon this old shepherd boy, I thought, 'Okay, now here is something new to learn about.' I decided to stay and the old shepherd boy didn't send me away.

"It was a nice place to stay, too. It was on a beautiful open hillside where the sun was often warm and the grazing was plentiful. I liked it here very much as I had not lived in a place like this before with my old herd. We had lived more in the upper areas where the air was cold and moss was often our food. We would come down to this area only in the coldest of months, but never did we stay.

"There was only one rule here: be as a goat would be, but do not act aggressively to the shepherd. If you did, there would surely be some whacks of a staff and banishment from the herd.

"I thought about the rule and decided that yes, I could do this. So I took this herd as my own and I stayed with them for a long time.

"*I spent many days watching the old shepherd boy as he would tend to his herd and to his life. I thought it must be very lonely for him to not have a herd of his own, but he did not seem to cry out for another of his own kind.*

"*I often would approach the shepherd, and he would pat me if I let him, and sometimes he would offer me a chewy fruit to share, but rarely anything else.*"

"*As seasons went by, the old shepherd boy grew weak. He headed his flock down the hillside toward that place that goats like me never went to. Since I was now a part of his flock, I followed the old boy and waited often as he stumbled on the rocks. At times I would let him hold onto me to steady himself, but he did not like to depend on me that way. The sun was warm and the smell of the air was light as the sound of hooves and ground and an occasional clank of a goat bell followed us as we walked. I wondered what it would be like to leave the hillside as I hurried along. I did not want to miss anything.*"

"*As we entered the village where the others of his herd lived, I saw a wondrous sight. Not only were there more shepherds of many sizes and kinds, but there were many wonderful smells. Activities surrounded me, but I stayed with the flock and followed our boy to a place near the other side of this wonderful village. Once there, the boy entered a small hole in the hillside and did not reappear. I grazed in the grassy areas, and I grazed on top of the hole he went into, and I watched and watched and listened.*

"*Another shepherd boy came out daily to tend to us. He milked who needed milking, he fed the kids who needed extra and he patted me, if I let him. But then he too would go back into the hole in the hillside and things would be as before.*

"*I liked the village and explored a little, but piles of branches kept me from straying too far (here he indicated a fence). It was a very busy place, but busy or not, I grew tired of this kind of existence. I missed the old shepherd boy and I missed the hillside even more. I decided that because the boy had not returned for so long, he surely must have forgotten about us. This was a sad thought for me to think and I was surprised that I was thinking it at all. I decided that I should return to that where I had come from, so over the pile of branches I went and slowly I walked back up the hillside.*

"The hillside had not changed much at all. The hot day flowers were in bloom now and gave me something to graze upon while I thought about my life. I pondered why the old shepherd boy, who seemed to love his flock so much, would go back to a herd and live in a hole? Even though he smelled like a goat and had lived with the goats, it was clear that he did not think like a goat about the way life should be. I decided then to stop thinking about the old boy, and I ventured further up into the hillside in search of my own first herd, whom I had left behind some years back.

"I was lonely. I cried. A goat needs a herd.

"My experience was growing near to its end, and this was a happy thing for me. I knew, as I always had, that at one point I would return to that misty, open place that I barely remembered as a kid. And even though the memory was vague, as it always had been, the feelings of it were plentiful. It was a place of warmth and herd and Knowing. It was a place of safety, happiness and review. It was a place of beginning and ending and beginning yet again. It was a place of always, and I was soon on my way.

"I lay on the hillside with my old body, looking towards the sky. I listened to the birds, sniffed the flowers that grew near my head and took one last gasp of warm sun air. I held that breath, but not because I could not expel it. I held that last breath because the beauty of what I was seeing took my breath away. The vision of my ending was the most beautiful sight I had ever seen.

"Brilliant sunshine enveloped me and I felt as light as the cool, spring air. Misty swirls curled around my body and

lifted me into the sunlight. Hums and tinkling sounds entered my head and little, sparkling fairies led me to that open space that I had remembered as a kid. There, amongst the softest of green spring grasses, I found myself with old shepherd boy gazing at me fondly. I let him pat me and he helped me to my feet. We shared a chewy fruit and we looked out over the flock. I knew that I was no longer on the hillside. I knew that I was in my new beginning, again.

"My experience with my old shepherd boy has been plentiful. If old shepherd boy takes a new beginning, sometimes I follow behind. After all, this is what a goat most assuredly does. And if I take a new beginning without my old shepherd boy, then sooner or later we meet, yet again. Before this new beginning, I followed my boy. I followed him to you, for that is who you are. Did you know that? Did you see it in my eyes? Did you see it in your own?

"Time here is not measured as it is in your space. Time here is measured by experience. My old shepherd boy is an experience that I have chosen to repeat... An experience that is worth repeating... An experience that I will look forward to again. Remember this truth, The Truth of Arturo, the Greatest Goat of All, for this is the experience that we share.

*"There will **always** be many endings for us, so that new beginnings can begin. I will follow you to the places you lead me, and I will wait for you to once again follow me. This is the way of goats. This is the way we are.*

"And, I say to you now 'Baahhhh,' so that you will know where I am ⌣ just over here, not far away.

"Close your eyes and you can still see me."

⌇

Epilogue …

Do Not Stand At My Grave and Weep

Do not stand at my grave and weep,
I am not there, I do not sleep.

I am a thousand winds that blow,
I am the softly falling snow.
I am the gentle showers of rain,
I am the fields of ripening grain.

I am in the morning hush,
I am in the graceful rush
Of beautiful birds in circling flight.
I am the star-shine of the night.

I am in the flowers that bloom,
I am in a quiet room.
I am in the birds that sing,
I am in each lovely thing.

Do not stand at my grave and cry,
I am not there ∼
I did not die.

–Author Unknown

Appendix 1

In honour and memory of the animals written about in this book, the animal service organizations listed here are graciously accepting donations in their names, or in memory of your own companion animal.

Your contributions will go directly toward the ongoing care, feeding, shelter and veterinary expenses for animals rescued from abuse or abandonment, as well as for injured or orphaned wildlife.

In Memory of Sheldon:

The Shetland Sheepdog Club of Northern California is a non-profit rescue operation. It was founded to help abandoned and surrendered Shelties in need of new homes. Rescue volunteers provide foster care for the dogs while appropriate new homes are identified. Often, these shelties have lived a life of abuse or neglect, so a rescue dog's foster home may be his first experience in a stable, caring environment.

SSCNC is an all-volunteer operation funded entirely by tax-deductible donations, adoption and placement fees, and fund raising efforts. An average of 60-70 Shelties who need new homes, are handled each year. Donated funds are allocated to cover veterinary care, phone calls, shelter adoption fees and advertising.

SSCNC Sheltie Rescue
5264 Keystone Dr.   510-728-9411
Fremont, CA 94536   24-hour hot-line
http://www.wetware.com/sheltie_rescue
E-mail: fugitpl@HPD.Abbott.com

In Memory of Tissy, Vincent, Plattie and Bela:

National Association of Potbelly Pigs of America

A 501(c)3 non-profit organization, NAPPA is the oldest potbelly pig service organization in the United States, and supports pet pig owners worldwide. Volunteers create a monthly newsletter and maintain an award winning website, both containing vital healthcare information for keeping pet pigs healthy and happy.

The NAPPA Memorial Fund uses your tax-deductible donation to help initiate new educational projects for the general public, potbellied pig pet owners, veterinarians, shelters and breeders.

NAPPA Memorial Fund

385 Muttart Road   920-725-5781
Neenah, WI 64781
            http://www.petpigs.com/nappa.htm
            E-mail: nappa@nappanet.com

In Honour of Clue and Chrissy Pig,

In Memory of Dudley, Molly, and Montana's Rose:

The Pet Loss Support Hotline at Cornell University

One of the leading veterinary universities in the world, Cornell College of Veterinary Medicine has recognized how pets often occupy a place in our lives akin to other family members. This in itself makes their death a time of deep emotions and sadness.

Trained by a professional grief counsellor, the volunteer veterinary student staff at The Pet Loss Hotline is there to help pet owners deal with the grief suffered when a companion animal dies.

This very special sector of Cornell's veterinary department, directed by Dr. Leslie Appel, DVM, believes that "having someone to turn to, someone who will listen, may be the first step to healing."

Literature regarding pet loss and grief is maintained by the hotline and is available to callers at their request.

Tax-deductible donations go directly toward such things as the cost of producing and mailing information packets, stamps, sympathy cards, and phone bills. Contributions are also used to help train new volunteers for the hotline, and to sponsor speakers who are well-versed in grief and pet loss.

Pet Loss Support Hotline
Companion Animal Hospital   607-253-3932
Box # 35   6-9 p.m. Tues-Thurs.
College of Veterinary Medicine
Cornell University
Ithaca, NY 14850-6401
     http://www.vet.cornell.edu/public/petloss/
     E-mail: petloss@cornell.edu

In Honour of Gilby, Comanche and the Wild Mustangs:

Institute of Range and the American Mustang

A non-profit corporation, IRAM was founded in 1988 by Dayton O. Hyde, whose mission was to give freedom and a quality of life to America's wild horses.

Several hundred wild horses run free on the 11,000-acre sanctuary in the Black Hills of South Dakota, which is also home to coyotes, cougar, mule deer, elk, wild turkeys and peregrine falcons.

Looking much as it did centuries ago, the sanctuary attracts visitors from all over the world, who come to see and photograph wild horses in large herds, against a backdrop of spectacular scenery.

Your tax-deductible donation goes toward the ongoing care of the sanctuary's wild mustangs and the purchase of more land upon which they may run freely.

Institute of American Mustang
P.O. Box #998   800-252-6652
Hot Springs, SD 57747   605-745-5955
http://222.gwtc.net/~iram
E-mail: iram@gwtc.net

In Memory of Millie:

Midwest Farm Animal Rescue

This tax-deductible, non-profit organization is dedicated to the rescue and rehabilitation of abused, abandoned and unwanted farm animals. Sixty-two animals currently reside on 100 acres of land, where they have life-long sanctuary.

"We receive and rescue animals from many situations ... animals that have been raised as pets, such as potbelly pigs and goats that end up at slaughter auctions because they are unwanted." (Reprinted from website.)

The dedicated all-volunteer staff provides each rescued animal the opportunity to live out its life free from further abuse and neglect. Each animal receives veterinary care, proper nutrition, and consistent interaction with kind, caring humans. Healthy and well-adjusted animals are adopted out to loving homes under strict guidelines.

Education, sponsorship programs, and volunteer opportunities all are a part of MFAR's efforts to promote compassion and sensitivity toward farm animals.

Midwest Farm Animal Rescue
P.O. Box #94   715-455-1506
Prairie Farm, WI 54762
http://www.mfar.org
E-mail: ANYTHING@mfar.org
See Appendix 2 for sanctuary donation ideas.

In Memory of Freeway, Avalanche and Morgan:

Guardians of Animals

Solely devoted to offering low-cost neutering and spaying for cats and dogs in Central New York, Guardians provides this service through its network of dedicated volunteers.

"Friends of Animals" spaying and neutering certificates are honoured by a select group of veterinarians, and your donation goes toward the offering of additional subsidies to pet owners who can not afford the discounted prices.

Donations to this program help relieve the needless suffering caused by pet overpopulation.

Guardians of Animals
P.O. Box #698   315-656-7590
Fayetteville, NY 13066
http://home.earthlink.net/~bkoren
E-mail: chapmancfm@hotmail.com

In Memory of Duchess:

The Duchess Fund

A 501(c)3 non-profit corporation dedicated to helping improve and extend the quality of life for pet pigs globally. With the collection of health records of potbelly pigs, the Duchess Fund sustains an on-line medical database, accessible world wide, for veterinarians and other animal health care providers to access. As of printing, seven veterinary medical universities have donated *all* of their pet pig records for inclusion, along with the veterinary records from pet pig owners around the world. More come on board daily.

"Neuter and Spay" videos are being produced for veterinary professionals who are unfamiliar with the most current techniques used for pet pigs, along with other

educational videos and information gathered from leading pet pig veterinarians nationwide. With the help of
the World Wide Web, the planet has become a smaller
place in which to live, and pet pig medical information is
now far less elusive than in years past. This will truly
revolutionize the veterinary world's ability to successfully
treat pet pigs.

The Duchess Fund
408 14th Street SW   813-641-1278
Ruskin, FL 335   Fax 813-645-1625
http://www.duchessfund.org
E-mail: Lordsmom@prodigy.net

In Memory of Randolph and J.R.:
Kalamazoo Animal Rescue
A 501(c)3 non-profit organization founded in 1991,
this special group is funded solely by private donations.
The animals are provided with all necessary veterinary
care from the time they arrive, and age allowing, all are
neutered or spayed prior to adoption.
Animals are placed with volunteer foster families who
open their homes to animals in need. Under caring, nurturing supervision, each animals' personality traits are
considered so adoption coordinators can match the animals with suitable permanent families.
Education is paramount to KAR and they assist in public education for the betterment of animals everywhere.

Kalamazoo Animal Rescue
P.O. Box #3295   616-349-2325
Kalamazoo, MI 49003
http://www.kalamazooanimalrescue.org
E-mail: kar@kalamazooanimalrescue.org

In Memory of Tom, Tiffany, Oreo and Sundancer:

Friends of Animals

An international, 501(c)3 non-profit, membership organization founded over three decades ago, FOA works to protect animals from cruelty, abuse and institutionalized exploitation.

Worldwide, FOA helps to protect and preserve animal habitats, and to foster a compassionate relationship between people and the animals of the world.

FOA supports local "Neuter and Spay" programs through participating veterinarians, who in turn offer their professional surgical services at a special discounted rate.

Donations are tax-deductible, and you may specify that yours to be put toward further subsidizing neuter or spay certificates for those who can't afford the discounted price.

This program helps ease the suffering caused by the overpopulation of dogs and cats.

Friends of Animals
777 Post Road   203-656-1522
Darien, CT 06820
http://friendsofanimals.org
E-mail: contact@friendsofanimals.org

In Memory of Aba and Phoebe:

Maryland Council for Special Equestrians

A 501(c)3 non-profit organization, MCSE is a therapeutic riding group that uses horses as an integral part of the rehabilitation process. Founded in 1988, this center treats human patients of all ages with a wide range of disabilities.

Within a safe, respectful and pleasant environment, this organization allows people with disabilities the opportunity to participate in an enjoyable activity. It also provides patients with many physical benefits such as improved balance and coordination, greater strength and muscle control, and increased range of motion, while enriching the quality of life of all participants.

"Our goal is to assist each person in achieving his or her maximum level of independence, while improving the general health and well-being of each rider." (Reprinted from Mission Statement.)

Under the supervision of a riding instructor and therapist, specially trained horses and riders learn to work as a team. Many times, these working therapeutic teams even enter competitions. One example is Bayou, a 35-year-old quarter horse who, with his mounts, has won more gold medals at the Special Olympics than any other horse in Maryland.

Fun, fitness and special bonds are all formed here, fostered within the sphere of "therapy."

Maryland Council for Special Equestrians
2501 Frederick Road   410-418-4300
Catonsville, MD 21228
http://www.bcpl.net/~gharris/ther.html
E-mail: tfram@home.com
See Appendix 2 for donation ideas.

In Memory of Lucky:

Mission: Wolf

A non-profit organization, this peaceful refuge for wolves is located in the remote mountains of Colorado. They do not promote wolves as pets.

Your tax-deductible donation goes toward their food, fencing and the purchase of more land upon which the wolves can roam freely, without persecution.

This all-volunteer staff of dedicated people tends to

the needs of the wolves daily, providing them with food, water, living space, companionship and privacy. Fence building is a year-round project, and a primitive visitor center provides visitors and volunteers with hands-on working experience with the wolves.

In an effort to stimulate people's caring and respect of nature, and to ensure the wolf's survival in America's wild lands, socialized "ambassador" wolves travel nationwide each year. By allowing people to look into the wild, yellow eyes of a wild wolf, this educational tour helps dispel myths and enhance participant's respect for nature.

The sanctuary also offers the possibility of academically accredited internship for students working toward a degree in environmental education, wildlife management, natural resources or veterinary medicine.

Mission: Wolf
P.O. Box #211   719-746-2919
Silver Cliff, CO 81249   or 802-888-3130
http://www.indra.com/fallline/mw
E-mail: peggy@plainfield.bypass.com

In Memory of Spike and Friends:

Pillar Pigs of the Community

Providing rescue, shelter and adoption services for abandoned or abused potbelly pigs. This organization also provides veterinary treatment for pigs-in-need, as well as educational opportunities for pet pig owners and potential pet pig owners.

Nationally, Pillar Pigs has tenaciously defended pigs as pets, and has worked tirelessly to insure that backyard breeders are held accountable to the laws governing the sale of pet pigs within the State of Florida, while helping local governments rewrite antiquated zoning laws by providing accurate and current information on pet pigs versus domestic pigs, for which outdated laws were originally written.

Although your monetary donation is not tax deductible, it will go toward helping the pigs within their associated sanctuaries to provide a quality, nurturing life for as long as each rescued pig lives there. Stringent adoption procedures are required by Pillar Pigs, in an effort to ensure that any pig adopted out to a new home will never find themself in need of rescuing again.

Membership with Pillar Pigs is available, and includes a quarterly newsletter full of timely events, association news, and sanctuary additions and adoptions.

Pillar Pigs of the Community
Barbara Baker   813-641-1278
408 14th Street SW   Fax 813-645-1625
Ruskin, FL 33570
Email: Lordsmom@prodigy.net
See Appendix 2 for sanctuary donation ideas.

In Memory of Kody:

The Pig Placement Network

An adoption service for pet pigs, PPN is part of the "Society for Advancement of Pet Pigs," a non-profit corporation. Ross Mill Farm & Piggy Camp, is a foster care facility for PPN, housing 40-70 rescued potbelly pigs while they hope for and await a new, loving, permanent home.

"As with all pets, potbellied pigs can lose their homes or become abandoned. We strive to bring together potbellied pigs and people in order to improve and enrich the lives of not only deserving pets, but their new owners as well." (Reprinted from Mission Statement.)

Volunteers work closely with pet pig owners, shelters, veterinarians and the general public to provide education about pigs as pets. They actively recruit and educate prospective pig parents before mating an adoptable pig to a new home.

PPN maintains a descriptive list of pet pigs that are up for adoption, some of which are young, old, or have disabilities or special needs. Their goal is to make a successful match with new, adoptive parents so that the pig never needs rescuing again.

The Pig Placement Network
PO Box 538   856-468-0665
Sewell, NJ 08080
        http://www.pigplacementnetwork.com
        http://www.rossmillfarm.com
        E-mail: Pigadopt@aol.com
See Appendix 2 for sanctuary donation ideas.

In Memory of Ming and Pasha:

Popcorn Park Zoo

A 501(c)3 non-profit organization operating under the auspices of the Associated Humane Societies, Popcorn Park is the only federally licensed rescue zoo of its kind in the United States.

Established in 1977 for the sole purpose of providing a refuge for sick, handicapped, injured, abused and abandoned animals that can not be returned to their natural habitat, over 200 animals now live on in spacious surroundings in the heart of scenic Pine Barrens, in southern New Jersey.

"Among the many attractions at Popcorn Park are a mighty African elephant, beautiful Bengal and Siberian tigers, regal African lions, mountain lions, and American black bears, all housed in large and comfortable compounds. The numerous species of animals found here attest to the diversity of animals

that have been in need of help and have found refuge at Popcorn Park." (Reprinted from website.)

Your tax-deductible donation enables Popcorn Park to maintain a low admission policy and the highest-quality care available for their animals. They receive no federal, state or local funding of any kind.

Popcorn Park Zoo
Humane Way   609-693-1900
P.O. Box #43
Forked River, NJ 08731
                http://www.popcornpark.org
                Email: njhumane@aol.com

In Memory of Squirrel, Samantha, McMurphy, Norman, Nike & Kismet:

KittyCorner of CNY Inc.

A 501(c)3 non-profit foster care facility for cats, KittyCorner is run under the loving care of Deb and Linda Young, sisters who are both school librarians, and who have opened their home to cats-in-need.

Their mission is to take in cats who've been thrown away by people, and find loving homes where they'll be cherished members of the family. The cats are provided with shelter, vet care and lots of love and understanding until the right person comes along.

With the help of volunteers, KittyCorner provides daily, caring human interaction with each cat in their care. They also provide veterinary care, which often includes neutering and spaying.

"Once a cat enters our program, we take lifetime responsibility. We will take the cat back at anytime if the adopter can't keep it for any reason. No cat ever need be homeless again." (Reprinted from Mission Statement.)

Your tax-deductible donation goes toward veterinary care, food bills and information packets for prospective adoptive families.

KittyCorner of CNY
P.O. Box #182   315-457-4420
Liverpool, NY 13088-0182
315-457-4420
> http://www.kittycorner.org
> Email: catresq@kittycorner.org
> See Appendix 2 for sanctuary donation ideas.

In Memory of Wild Dog and Samson:
Keepers of the Wild

This non-profit sanctuary is deeply dedicated to the rescuing of endangered species. The preservation and protection of these wonderful, exotic animals is paramount in their hearts and minds. For many of the animals, this is their last chance for a life of peaceful coexistence with man ... Their last hope.

Providing a clean, safe and loving environment for over 100 exotic animals, including lions, tigers, leopards, jaguars, cougars, wolves and other wonderful animals, this organization cares for these wild animals with veterinarians experienced with exotics.

"When rescued, these animals become a part of our family. We love, nourish and care for them as if they were our children. Because in reality, they are."

Educating the public about the beauty and grace of these exotic creatures, so that man can learn to live in harmony with animals of the wild, is the reason Keepers of the Wild presents it's animals to the world, via the World Wide Web.

Keepers of the Wild
HC 37 Box 980   877-456-4004
Kingman, AZ 86413   Toll Free
520-767-4004
http://www.keepersofthewild.org
Email: keepers@citlink.net

In Memory of Melvin the Large:

The Tusk & Bristle ⁓ Center for the Porcine Arts

This center is home and sanctuary for about 50 rescued potbelly pigs. Many of them have come to live there after their suffering terrible abuses or abandonment. Others have been given up by families who were not committed to their pet. And some have come to live here after their loving humans fell ill and were unable to care for them any more.

No matter the pig's story, each one is provided veterinary care, potbelly pig feed, fresh produce and 14 or more acres upon which to roam, graze and to be a pig.

Personal attention is given daily to each of the pigs, who come when called by name. Each shares safe, secure and warm housing during the long, cold days of northern winters, which last about five months of the year.

Carol, a wildlife rehabilitator, and her husband, Jim, a high school science teacher, are sole providers for the pigs, funding their veterinary care, feed, fencing, housing and heating themselves.

The Tusk & Bristle
% Carp Cove Press   315-652-4964
P.O. Box #2991   (at Animal Wellness)
Liverpool, NY 13089-2991
E-mail: eiswald@mciworld.com
See Appendix 2 for sanctuary donation ideas.

In Memory of Arturo ∽ the Greatest Goat of All:

Lollypop Farm and Petting Zoo

Encompassing 133 acres of scenic Central New York, near Rochester, the Humane Society at Lollypop Farm was founded in the late 1950s by former director Ray Naramore. This very special farm was established in a unique way, as an effort to promote animal appreciation and responsible pet-ownership through education. Although criticized by colleagues at the time, Naramore developed a way to educate the public and draw them to the animal shelter, where he then made learning about animals fun. Quickly, Lollypop Farm has grown in popularity as a family attraction. Today kids of all ages still gather to watch, feed, photograph and interact with a variety of domestic and exotic creatures.

Sponsor of Lollypop Farm, the Humane Society of Rochester takes in over 12,000 unwanted, abandoned or abused animals every year. Through careful screening, these animals are placed in loving homes with responsible owners whenever possible. The staff and volunteers are proud of the fact that they have one of the highest adoption rates in the country.

Contributions are tax-deductible and go toward providing food, veterinary care and shelter for the animal residents and rescues at Lollypop Farm, some of which include dogs, cats, ferrets, guinea pigs, hamsters, goats, rabbits, potbelly pigs, horses, llamas, doves, ducks, geese, ponies, and sheep.

Lollypop Farm

P.O. Box #299	1-888-Lollypop
99 Victor Road	Toll Free
Fairport, NY 14450-0299	Fax 716-425-4183

http://www.Lollypop.org
E-mail: info@Lollypop.org

Appendix 2

Whether they are found at a sanctuary, a shelter or an organization devoted solely to the welfare of animals, the people behind these operations are usually selfless when it comes to those in their charge. Too often they are unsung heroes, giving all they have to ensure that animals they tend to never suffer again.

Endless hours are spent nursing back to health those that are sick, weak or maimed. Day in and day out, they work tirelessly to give the animals a clean, healthy environment. Often they are found emptying their own pockets and resources to pay for food, shelter, bedding and healthcare for those they have rescued.

If you would like to donate goods or your time to a specific animal shelter or one of the sanctuaries mentioned in this book, or if you would like to donate helpful goods to one of the Appendix 1 animal service organizations in memory of an animal written about here, your gift will be appreciated more than you can know. The following is a list of items that are always in need:

- *Animal Feed*: Specific to each species, gift certificates can be acquired from the feed stores the shelter/sanctuary buys from, allowing your monetary gift to be spent specifically on a gift of food. Or, donations of grocery store produce, no longer saleablefor humans, is a wonderful gift of nutrition for all animals.

- *Bedding Supplies*: Gifts such as blankets, straw, or radiant heaters are always in need. Radiant heaters heat only the animals and not the air around them, making them very safe for barn use.

• _Cleaning Supplies:_ Always a necessity when housing animals, gifts of items such as bleach, disinfectant, paper towels, sponges, buckets and mops are always appreciated. Also important are litter, wood shavings, sawdust, litter boxes, scoopers and rakes or manure picks for the larger animals.

• _Fencing and Housing:_ A gift of supplies to construct sturdy fencing, such as chain link, hog panel, welded wire, posts and hardware. Dog igloos, port-a-huts or animal carriers are always in demand. Please consider small wooden buildings which can be used to house either animals or supplies, also.

• _Healthcare:_ A gift certificate to the veterinary animal hospital that your chosen shelter/sanctuary uses. Or, if you are a professional veterinary healthcare practitioner, a donation of your time and services to a sanctuary.

• _Holistic Healthcare:_ A gift of, or a gift certificate for, homeopathic remedies or flower essences. Both therapies are highly effective, low cost and have no side effects, giving caregivers another approach to dealing with emotional trauma and first-aid situations while working in conjunction with their regular vets.

• *Neuter or Spay:* A donation for this service to the shelter/sanctuary of your choice helps ensure that adoptable rescued animals can go to their new homes already altered. This gift makes sure no offspring are produced, adding to the current over-population of unwanted pets.

• *Office Supplies:* Stamps, paper, envelopes, help in the office, etc. Running any kind of organization means paperwork of some kind, especially for non-profit groups who must file quarterly reports.

• *Sponsorship:* Many shelters and sanctuaries allow you to sponsor an animal, providing you a wonderful opportunity to help one particular animal-in-need. For those who cannot adopt an animal, this is a great alternative. Riding centers appreciate the donation of calm horses and tack.

• *Time:* The gift of your time, to help at a shelter or sanctuary near you, can be the most rewarding donation of all. Helping to clean, care for, nurture and love the animals recovering from physical or emotional trauma is undeniably one of the most enlightening and rewarding experiences you may ever have.

• *Toys:* Never under estimate the healing power of a good time.